WHITE PAPERS FOR WHITE AMERICANS

WHITE PAPER

OR WHITE AMERICANS

CALVIN C. HERNTON

DOUBLEDAY & COMPANY, INC.

GARDEN CITY, NEW YORK, 1966

LIBRARY OF CONGRESS CATALOG CARD NUMBER 66–12244
COPYRIGHT © 1966 BY CALVIN C. HERNTON
ALL RIGHTS RESERVED
PRINTED IN THE UNITED STATES OF AMERICA
FIRST EDITION

This book is dedicated
to my son Antone
and
to the memory of Dr. Fritz Pappenheim
who was my teacher and friend

ACKNOWLEDGMENTS

Portions of "Grammar of the Negro Revolution" have appeared in the *Negro Digest* under the title of "Is There Really a Negro Revolution?" and "Stranger in Babylon," in an altered form, has appeared in *Présence Africaine*. Part of "The Debt I Owe" was taken by *Dissent* for use before the book was to appear.

This book was not written without the aid, in one way or another, of certain persons who should be mentioned here. They are Professor Harlan Joye and Margaret St. Denis, Charles Johnson, Steve Cannon, and Tom Dent.

C.C.H.

I am nobody
A red sinking autumn sun
Took my name away

RICHARD WRIGHT

CONTENTS

PART ONE   WHITE PAPER

1. The Debt I Owe   3

PART TWO   ANOTHER MAN DONE GONE

2. And You, Too, Sidney Poitier!   53

3. Grammar of the Negro Revolution   71
   ILLUSION AND REALITY

   POSTSCRIPT
   Another Man Done Gone:
   the Death of Malcolm X   97

4. Blood of the Lamb   105
   THE ORDEAL OF JAMES BALDWIN

   POSTSCRIPT
   A Fiery Baptism   129

5. Stranger in Babylon   149
   REFLECTIONS ON THE MARCH
   ON WASHINGTON

PART ONE

WHITE PAPER

My time done come
I got to pay the debt I owe
FROM A SPIRITUAL

CHAPTER I

THE DEBT I OWE

On important holidays and especially at Christmas, the buses and trains leaving the North and heading South are heavy-laden with what seems like an infinite assortment of black people. They are young and old, good, bad, indifferent. There are children among them; some are very black, others very light, and still others of all the shades and hues in-between. There are women, young, old, pretty, ugly, fat, lean, short, tall, of all sizes and shapes. There are those who are completely ignorant or semiliterate, as well as school teachers, doctors, social workers, skilled laborers, and technicians.

Every year they go up and down the country like refugees of some dark and embattled republic, like an endless caravan of ambivalent migrants torn between homeland and newland, continually returning to see

3

loved ones and friends and relatives, returning to memories that ache and yet somehow warm the heart.

Last Christmas, I too found myself in Pennsylvania Station, standing in line, waiting to purchase a ticket that would take me back, deep into the recesses of the "Down-Home Country." Standing there in that long line, I realized something I had never thought about before. Everywhere, at all the ticket windows, at the information booth, in the snack bar, on the benches and throughout the entire station there were hordes and hordes of black faces. Three out of four persons were Negro. How strange this must have seemed to the few whites who were scattered among us. I saw them glancing and staring like perplexed puppies—"Where are all these Negroes going?" They must have known where we were going, but *why* must have been the question. The philosophical *why* caused them to stand and gaze at us with curious and puzzled faces. How can white people possibly know or understand, in the face of the much publicized anti-Negro bigotry in the South, the secret longings in the hearts, souls, and minds of Negroes that pull them back down to that terrible place, year after year, season after season?

The Negroes were dressed up! They had on suits, ties, nice shoes, new dresses, smart-looking coats and, no doubt, clean underwear. They were busy talking. They appeared excited and enthused about their journey homeward. Some of them were, although quite well-behaved, a little tipsy. Their eyes were aglow as if they were putting something over on someone. Their tongues suffused the lofty dome of Penn Station with what I knew to be the conversation content, syntax and speech pattern of Down-Home Negroes. Their posture, their gestures, their stance, despite attempts at being hippy-dippy, were those of southern Negroes. I looked down at myself. I had not thought of dressing up. I wore corduroy trousers, a workman's flannel shirt, and my favorite leather jacket on the back of which the crooked, illegible lettering of a four-year-old child was barely visible. In my hip pocket was a notebook and in my notebook was a sharpened pencil. I felt alone, out of place, alienated. I was not going back down South to impress anybody. Although I did not abhor the idea, I was not really going back to have a ball. I was going back to try, as best I could, to resolve a conundrum. Rather than jubilant, or vainly proud, I was melancholy and pensive. I had to find out if I was through with the South, if it was through with me, if I was through with my relatives whom I love, my mother, my in-laws, my grandmother sauntering toward a centennial of life and joy and struggle on this earth. Essentially I was a little afraid. As I stood there in the station like that (naked, so to speak), an existential insight took possession of my imagination.

All except a very few of the Negroes I had known

and seen in the North were exactly like those in whose midst I was now standing. They were, like myself, migrants from the South. But there, the similarity between me and them ended. Thousands and thousands of southern Negroes come to various parts of the North with their woes and their children. They bear more children, and their children bear children. But everything else remains the same, they do not change. Except for a better job and perhaps a more adequate house in which to live, they remain *southern* Negroes even unto the second generation. Most of them might as well still be living in South Carolina or Georgia or wherever they have come from.

I think of Newark, New Jersey, where the round of daily life for the mass of Negroes is impossible to distinguish from that of Negroes in any ghetto south of the Potomac River. Specifically on Sunday, some Negroes in Newark act the same as others do in, say, Huntsville, Alabama. All day long they go to church. Baptist, Methodist, and Holy Roller. The men put on their suits and ties and their shined shoes, the women put on solid white or black dresses. They go to Sunday school, stay for the morning service, then return home and eat southern fried chicken, collard greens, and corn bread, and at night they attend service again. Throughout the day there is quartet singing, "battles of music," gospels and spirituals. On the Negro radio stations, and some white ones that cater to the Negro market, there is gospel music all day, and the announcers with their thick Negro dialects are difficult to understand if one is not from down South. The teenagers get "sharp," and after church they throng the sidewalks and street corners. They do not do anything, they have nowhere to go. They just mill around, being sharp on Sunday, and whistle at girls and passers-by. Those who own or who have the use of automobiles ride through the ghetto, picking up girls and joking with those hanging out on the block. This is Newark, New Jersey, where thousands of Negroes who have migrated from the South are still down South.

The overwhelming majority of southern Negroes who relocate in Newark or Harlem or Chicago or Washington, D.C., never really leave the South. They migrate physically but do not migrate spiritually or culturally. Nothing happens to them intellectually as a consequence of geographically coming North. They still think and speak categorically of white people as "crackers." The hate is still there, and so is the fear. They might work with and move in and among whites and even exchange polite words, but in all of this they maintain a rigid sociopsychological distance. Their souls and minds remain chained to the Down-Home Country. They are not chained to the land because they have no land. They are not chained to any material structures of the South because they have no access to material structures except the bleak façades of the ghetto. Rather, it is the ethos of the southern ghetto and the folkways of the South in general that southern Negroes have internalized and which they seem to be incapable of purging from their psyches. When they reach the northern environment, instead of expanding and shedding the old baggage and reorienting themselves to a new life, they, in many instances, tighten up and look for the familiar, and what they find is nothing less than a replica of the Down-Home habitat, the northern ghetto.

Some of this is due to the fact that in the North Negroes are often forced to live in ghettos and are actually, however subtly, denied the pursuit of a new life. Just as frequently, however, the southern way of life has rendered the Negro incapable of *ever* making a philosophical transformation regardless of where he might go. The South is a psychocultural region of mixed personality determinants whose conflicting vectors completely immobilize the flexibility and continued growth of the psyche. On the one hand, the Negro is the exclusive product of ghetto life in the South—on the other hand, he is a general product of southern folkways. He has both worlds inside him, and he is loyal to both although he has only participated in one. He is, therefore, wedded to the entire South just as certainly as the white southerner. The Negro's hopes and fears, his embarrassments and guilts and sore spots, are southern. The fact that many ex-southern and southern Negroes are ashamed of the South or of some of its aspects reveals that they *love* it so much; it is HOME, the only home they will ever really know.

The fact that Negroes are alienated from the broader life of the South and its deeper mysteries does not frequently pull them away, but binds them ever more closely to the bosom of Down-Home. The South is the mother-matrix out of which and in which the Negro's mind has been fashioned; it is at the same time the festering ache in the republic of his heart. This, more than anything else, is why they go back.

So, I too took a trip back. Long before I reached the Tennessee town where I was born, I knew that what I saw, with both my mind and my eye, would determine whether or not this visit would be my last.

Entering Chattanooga, I was struck by the degree to which the city had changed. The train came into the city via a route quite unsuspected by me. I saw that old factories and plants (for Chattanooga is mainly an industrial center) had been demolished and sharp new ones had taken their places. I saw that many slum areas had been leveled and cleared. Modern structures, housing projects, and office buildings shone bright and as yet unsoiled in the winter sun. There were new bridges and freeways and turnpikes, and more were under construction. Streets within the city had been widened. The north side of Chattanooga, where great smoke stacks rose up to the sky and railroad yards laden with cargo furrowed the land, looked crystal and fresh as if in some futuristic era. And from the heights of East Ridge clear across town to the southernmost part of the city and beyond, a grand overhead freeway was being constructed.

In a way it was no surprise, for one is aware that as industrialization and city life become more of a fact in the South, sweeping technological innovations are the necessary concomitants. Characteristic of the South, however, is the tendency for southerners to separate the technological aspects of their world from its social or human morality, especially with reference to the Negro. I began to wonder to what extent the human aspects of their lives had kept or were keeping pace with the inspiring technological changes I saw everywhere.

In all the major southern cities (excluding those in Mississippi), desegregation is noticeable in the schools, in interstate transportation facilities, in the larger hotels and some eating establishments, and even in certain areas of employment. In the city where I was born I saw Negro women working as cashiers in a local supermarket that formerly employed only whites, except in the most menial jobs. I was impressed to find that even in the smaller towns and hamlets far more bus and train stations have dropped all visible signs of enforced segregation than one would expect.

Equally important, if not more so, is the beginning of change in the personal as well as public attitudes of whites toward the Negro. As I walked the streets, I was aware of not being stared at with as much hatred and as frequently as in the past. In department, drug, and food stores, I discerned an attitude on the part of some whites which approached authentic respect for me as a human being. Much of the change in attitude is taking place in, not all, but a great many of the white youth, noticeably in those who might have been or who are in the Armed Forces and those who attend schools outside the South. Their experiences in a desegregated atmosphere seem to be counteracting many of the prejudices and hateful emotions that they had internalized from a southern upbringing.

On the train down from New York, a white youth seated behind me touched my shoulder and extended his hand with obvious warmth, explaining that he was a Columbia University student and that he had been in the audience during a poetry reading in which I had participated. He moved up and sat with me and we talked. He had a thick southern accent, but not once did I discern the overt or hidden disrespect for the Negro that usually accompanies such an accent.

In a rural South Carolina town I witnessed an in-

cident where a group of white youths, who were waiting
outside a supermarket, came over to a Negro youth, who
also seemed to be waiting for someone, and began a
friendly conversation. The mother of the Negro youth
explained that more and more of this is taking place,
and that such a thing would not have happened a year
earlier. She further stated that whites in general were
referring to Negroes as "Mr." and "Mrs." more frequently
than they used to, and that, "Us Negroes are getting
where we can talk back or speak up to whites like men
and women without the crackers wanting to bash in our
heads or asking us, 'What did you say, Nigger?' and
we'd have to drop our heads and mumble, 'Nothing,' to
Miss Ann or to Mr. Charlie. Us black folks are getting
where we don't have to do that any more."

While one must recognize these and other changes in
the South which indicate that the trend will continue
on a more broad and intensive basis, I must also emphasize that the actual social status of the Negro in
general is in fact the same as it was ten years ago. By
and large Negroes are still without the ballot, still denied
equal job opportunities, still the victims of Jim Crow
and bigotry. Isolated incidents of token integration, human respect and kindness from whites are not yet the
rule but the exception. The young whites who are sym-
pathetic toward the Negro struggle constitute only a small
fraction of the total white population, and they are neither

statistically nor qualitatively in a position to uproot the intricate system of race hatred and human oppression that has been and is still one of the *foundations* of the "southern way of life."

The greatest change in the South is not a significant innovation in the sociopolitical status of the Negro. Nor is it any appreciable mitigation of southern hatred and inhumanity in the hearts of whites or in their actual behavior toward black people. Rather, it is the philosophical transformation, the *morale*, of a large portion of southern Negroes about alleviating their oppression. Formerly the Negro was handicapped by his own attitude regarding his status in the South. Largely, he believed that he was helpless, that protests and demonstrations and fighting back were useless, that "we Negroes just can't stick togther." This is changing. The Negro now has a new morality. He actually believes that he himself can wage a gradually successful fight and, indeed, overcome. Make no mistake, the great percentage of southern Negroes, especially the youth, know damn well that if some changes are taking place, it is almost solely because of *their* valiant struggle, of *their* bloodshedding and deaths, and not because of any good will or change of heart on the part of "white folks." The northern liberals and other whites who want to help would do well to take cognizance of this when they, whether intentionally or unconsciously, speak about the "role of liberal whites" in bringing about changes in the South, and when white southerners offer the hand of "friendship" to black youths.

Over and over again, I discerned, smoldering beneath the breath of the young blacks, a terrible hatred for southern, and some northern, whites who now—since the "revolution" seems to be unarrestable—offer their friendship, as if this would wipe out all the years of the Negro's toil and suffering. It goes against my emotions, but it seems to me that the cessation of centuries of being hated cannot wipe out overnight the welled-up desire to hate back. The young blacks do not want to shake hands and forget. They want revenge. The Negro youths know that they have been immeasurably crippled by centuries of racism in America, and, when freedom comes and even after, they are aware that the effects of racism will still be a hideous ghost taunting their minds, their souls, and their egos. God, along with Dr. Martin Luther King, might absolve the white folks. But, I am afraid, before significant numbers of contemporary black southern youth (not to mention those in the North) can ever love, they will first have to hate.

If the technological changes in the South were as slow and incomplete as those needed in the area of human relations, there would be but half of a turnpike, a fourth of a bridge, a third of a new plant, and so on. The only significant social innovation that the South has finally instituted on a broad scale is desegregation. But there is very little *integration*. I observed, for instance, that, with the exception of the state of Mississippi and a few more isolated places, the physical barriers in interstate and some local traveling facilities are completely down—there are no signs, no partitions, no separate baths or ticket windows. Yet, almost everywhere, blacks and whites huddle together in separate bundles. It was uncanny when I walked into the Greyhound station in Spartanburg, South Carolina, and saw no racial barriers whatever, to find blacks and whites sitting as far from one another as possible, like scared chickens. At that moment I was engulfed by a terrible sadness. It was as if the physical barriers were still there and, indeed, they were. The barriers were the people themselves. They had leaped out of the psyches of whites and blacks alike, and stood there in the station as firmly as if they had never been torn down but reinforced. *Segregation is at least as much a psychosomatic phenomenon as it is objectively physical.* To remove the concrete barriers is but half the job. It is similar to removing the bandages and leaving the sores alone to fester in pain.

More than one Negro told me that it was perhaps not a good thing for one or two Negro children to attend integrated—no, *desegregated*—schools because, ". . . . the Negro children are going to have to spend a year or more getting used to all those white children, and they won't have time to concentrate on their learning and will waste time." At one point I grew angry and made a sarcastic retort: "What do you think is going to happen to the poor white children, trying to get *used* to those black ones . . . ?"

For most southern Negroes and whites, associating with the opposite color constitutes an exotic experience fraught with nameless fears. Now that the physical barriers are coming down, Negroes and whites alike find it difficult to define their fears. It is not so much the fear of violence—both groups are accustomed to violence. It is not so much the fear of intermarriage. It is a fear in the mind, a fear of the psyche-self, a fear, if you please, of *pain* that will havoc the entire personality structure as a consequence of becoming *involved* with people of another color. Existential pain.

No matter how many objective barriers, political or economic, are brought down by the present strife, there will be no peace in the South until the corresponding subjective barriers in the personalities of blacks and whites are assailed, uprooted and flung to the ground. This pain must be undergone and mastered.

The old bigots and the new young racists are incapable of mastering such pain. The South will change but the bigots and racists will never change. They will have to die off or be killed. It is not a matter of "cultural lag." Rather than explaining or providing a frame of reference

16

for meaningful understanding and analysis of the South, the cultural lag formula serves to obfuscate the issues and mechanically to excuse the South for its reactionary institutions. Put away the sociological theories, all of them, and examine the South as a *thing* that is *there*.

The explicit and essential function of the southern way of life has been and is, with reference to human relations, the maintenance and promotion of systematic oppression of the Negro. When, over the years, the interlocking structures of Negro oppression became institutionalized into an ongoing system, that system was a *fait accompli,* never to change or evolve out of itself, but only to grow stronger within itself. For southern society, it was and still is a *positive* system. It may seem evil, wrong, and so on, to northerners and Negroes, but for a certain class of white southerners it is and was good, beneficial, and divine. The *existence* of the racist or bigot is bound, is indeed *condemned,* to this system. The southern way of life, here meaning Negro oppression, is the single, most important factor upon which the majority of southerners base their self-esteem. It is at once objective fact in his society and also the subjective order out of which he conceives the essence of his very being. Attack this system and you attack his sense of the *reality* of his person. A maniac kills for his sense of "well-being." Rarely do we cure or re-educate the maniac. He dies, gets killed, or we put him in an asylum. The racists and the bigots, save a few, have nothing to live for if their world crumbles. This is similar to a visceral need. Wipe out the system of Negro oppression in the South and you automatically destroy the racist's sense of well-being. Not only is the feeling of "personal worth" predicated upon inhumanity toward the Negro, but southern "manhood" and "white womanhood" seem to stem more from the southerner's conception, and treatment, of the Negro as a "nigger" than from any independent sense of dignity on the part of the racists.

In a very literal sense the racist, in ideology and in fact, *needs* "the nigger." Hatred for Negroes in the South is not a theoretical or an impersonal thing; it is a deep *intimate* emotion which constitutes a vital part of the everyday life of "white folks." Contrary to much contemporary sociological theory, the Negro is not an abstraction, not merely a generalization. Those who hate the Negro, hate him *carnally*. They hate him biologically: his smell, his color, his genitals, his features. Almost invariably the killing or mistreatment of a Negro by southern whites is not done in an objective, impersonal manner. The Negro's body is attacked and maimed. His flesh is beaten and violated in a most intimate and pornographic fashion, as if by a lover who has gone mad.

It is a well-established principle in modern psychology that when hatred becomes so personal, so carnal and intimate, the rage and fury of the hater is not only generated by revulsion for the hated but also by an alien desire to "love" the hated. By *alien*, I mean a desire that is socially and morally forbidden but which the person cannot rid himself of. He therefore must suppress it, thereby intensifying his agony to the point where it explodes in the most violent hatred for the forbidden object.

The Negro is torn between self-love and self-hate. This ambivalence is strictly a manifestation in the Negro of the "hate-love syndrome" with which whites are afflicted regarding their emotions toward black people. Why, for instance, during the current flurry of civil rights demonstrations in the South, are whites so eager to provoke physical violence? Specifically, in Selma, Alabama, as elsewhere, the desire for intimate contact with Negroes is perversely fulfilled in and through acts of tussling with and beating colored people. After all, any sensible person knows that the mere fact of Negroes marching is not going to achieve very much. In my opinion, the most objective response would be to let them march, ignore them. There are sufficient indications to assert that white southerners are, if not "in love" with Negroes, definitely emotionally involved with or "hung-up" on the black people who are bodily and psychologically in their midst.

Whites down South do not leave Negroes alone even when the Negroes, so to speak, remain in their place. *The fact is, southern whites and Negroes are more alike*

in every way, save skin color, than most of us are ac-
customed to believing. On the train going from New
York, once we were out of Washington, D.C., I noticed
a sight familiar to passenger trains in the South. Up and
down the train a Negro "conductor" followed close behind his white counterpart in goose-step fashion. Upon
reflection and deep scrutiny, it was amazing how similar
these two men were—their stances, their faces, the skin
of their chins toughened from years of shaving, their
mannerisms, their hands. The two men must have been
working together for decades. Of course, on one level,
they represented the traditional symbols of Mr. Charlie
and Uncle Tom. But on the human level, as sociocul-
tural products, they were twin brothers.

Earlier, outside Philadelphia, a young woman had
come to my seat and introduced herself, explaining that
she had been a student of mine when I taught social
sciences at a college in South Carolina. I did not remember her, but from her enthusiasm and the way she
talked about me, I knew she had been in my class. She
was light brown, petite, full of giggles and childish
blushes. She was "going back" to see relatives. Although
she had been in New Jersey for several years and was
a school teacher there, she was as if she had never
left the South, and, in every way that counted, she
had not. Her speech pattern, her outlook on life, her
inhibitions and general posture had not been tinted one

bit by coming North. When she started to express her
well-guarded sensitivity against whites and blacks associating with each other (I had been accompanied on the
train in New York by a white female companion, and
this no doubt was what had drawn her attention to me
in the first place!), I cut her short and she returned
to her seat. It has since dawned on me that had I been
farther down South and the color of the young woman's
skin white instead of brown, I might well have been
arrested (or worse) for associating with a "lily white
southern lady."

To wit, there are strong, intimate and terrible forces,
factors and conditions in the South which bind whites
and blacks together as one people just as the racist system
so painfully keeps them separated. Historically the South
has been described as a rural, tradition-directed society
with a culture rooted in the past and determined more
by folkways and blind customs than by law or technical
innovations. Despite the continuing disappearance of
agrarian life and the rise of cities, along with other industrial or technological changes, the southern people,
black and white, are to this day still a rural-minded, anti-
cosmopolitan, morally primitive type of people. Both
groups enjoy a slow pace of life, both are possessed by
a regional psychology which tends to make them in-
digenous-minded, semi-ignorant about the world, suspicious of "outsiders" and whatever is new. Most southern-

ers are creatures of the folkways where ingroupism, blind loyalty, and fear supersede openmindedness and preclude change. Except for the current change in the morale of southern Negroes regarding their oppression, the fundamental life or world outlook of blacks in the South is strikingly similar to that of southern whites. The stereotypes of "crackers" and "niggers" are much more than stereotypes. They are terms which describe and involve an interchangeable reality—the "southern way of life"—which constitutes, however separate, a *shared history* that is embedded in and has shaped the personalities of whites and blacks alike. Observe, for instance, how three historical experiences—religious fundamentalism, racism, and economic exploitation by the North—have wrought in the personalities of both blacks and whites a distorted, if not guilt-ridden sexuality, a hate-and-love ambivalence, and a pathological attitude regarding northerners. To speak realistically of "the southern mind" is to speak not only of the white, but of the black as well.

Contrary to what we are used to hearing, contrary to most sociological and psychological thought on the South, it is the *similarities* of blacks and whites, rather than the differences, that serve as fear-triggering mechanisms and prevent them from coming together under one moral and human order. Rather than the physical twoness of Negro and white in the South, it is their historical oneness that serves as the secret volcano of fear behind the visible and invisible barriers erected between them. The fact that many southern Negroes and whites go to great lengths in asserting their "differences" is an indication of the contrary. Racism and Jim Crow are, in this context, simply attempts to obliterate that part of the South, its true history, without which there would be no terror in our hearts when we speak of having a cup of coffee in a desegregated restaurant. The underlying magnets between whites and blacks in the South are the dynamics of fear that alienate them. Make no mistake, they will be alienated for a long time yet. They will be alienated not because they hate each other so much but because they love one another with such unspeakable guilt.

So, having been away for almost a decade, I returned to the region of my birth, my upbringing, my sorrows. It was as if I made a journey back into a dark territory of my own mind, back to some dark alley, to an incident under a house or to a forgotten experience in a weedy field long ago. I went back to memories, back to the twilight of first becoming a Negro or, if you prefer, becoming a "nigger." And, despite the changes that are definitely taking place in the South, nearly everywhere I went I saw the living manifestations of the Negro's "niggerhood," lingering and holding forth, stalking the black man's mind and world like a line of zombies without end.

The ghetto. If the Negro is ever to have a fair chance at a good and healthy life in this country, the ghetto existence must be utterly destroyed. As long as Negroes are forced to live in settings that are exclusively Negro, no matter how much advancement is made in civil rights, equal employment, school desegregation, and so on, the Negro's existence plus the way he looks at himself will continue to be something less than that of a human being. It must be understood once and for all, by blacks and whites, that the Negro's concept of himself as a "nigger" stems significantly from the fact that he *lives,* he sleeps and makes love and eats and raises children, all in a closed world. Throughout the South, not to mention the North, Negroes have lived and are living in outgroup habitats, separate and apart from the habitats of those who, from the viewpoint of the Negro, constitute the "ingroup" of the "outside world." No matter what Negroes achieve in the outside world, by the mere fact that there *is* this outside world, they will be afflicted by the knowledge on some level of consciousness that they are "different"; that in some way, however indefinable, they are still niggers. And this will hurt. It will damage one's self-esteem much in the same way as admitting a Negro to an "integrated" classroom, on the one hand, while, on the other, "segregating" him in the far corner of the room. To be "a part" of something and yet not to be conclusively included—this is alienation.

No one in America seems to understand the nature of the ghetto, or perhaps we understand it altogether too well. The clean ghetto is equally as cancerous as the dirty or the slum ghetto. The ghetto is an inbred sore. Whether it is composed of slum-ridden shanty dwellings or newly constructed housing projects, in time the physical and psychological effects of the ghetto are the same. The physical plants deteriorate, crime and other social ills set in, and the psychology of the inhabitants demoralizes to inferiority and self-hatred. The ghetto is not a community. It is a reservation site. It reduces the people from the status of human beings to that of domesticated livestock. The sore of the ghetto feeds upon itself. From the beginning, the ghetto is culturally and spiritually bankrupt. The inhabitants are so monolithic in morality, in artistic appreciation, in education, and in general social outlook, that little, if any, spontaneity and creativeness in living is possible. The objective and psychological condition of black people in America as inferior human beings cannot be completely rectified until the Negroes, all of them, engage themselves in a relentless and total assault upon that part of America known to them, in the slightest regard, as the "White World." It is the

exclusiveness of the white world or community that ultimately must be annihilated.

The police. Historically, one of the crucial functions
of the police in the South has been to gestapo and harass
the black ghetto. The existence and maintenance of the
ghetto has served to complement the above function of
the police. Largely, this situation continues to hold true
throughout the South today. One cannot begin to emphasize the extent of the brutality, the atrocities and
disrespectful acts committed against the Negro within
and without the ghetto by the white police. It is dangerous, for instance, for a Negro to be caught outside of
the ghetto at night. He runs the risk of being, if not
beaten, jailed on any of five hundred charges the cops
can dream up. This is especially so if the Negro is not
of the professional class. But even if he is, it is not
unlikely that he will be harassed and arrested. I recall
an incident that happened to a college professor in
Georgia. It was summer and the professor, vacationing,
was sitting in his front yard reading a book. The white
cops came up, insulted him, and jailed him on the charge
of "vagrancy." The harassment and acts of brutality do
not stop with just the males. Black women are ripe game
for disrespect and acts of assault by the police. Sexual
exploitation and downright rape are familiar crimes that

Negro women have to suffer from the white law enforcement agents.

That the police in the South have been and still are one of the main forces used to keep the Negro in his place is unmistakably illustrated in the use to which they are being put in the current southern civil rights struggle. The nature of the law has been and is, with reference to the Negro, nothing more than lawlessness against the Negro. The police are but another aspect of the racist system and its maintenance. Over the years more crimes have been committed in the South against Negroes than those that Negroes have actually committed throughout the nation.

The very existence of the "Negro community," the ghetto, is for the purpose of police exploitation not only in terms of intimidation and physical brutality, but also in terms of certain illegal traffics that are fostered upon the black ghetto by the white outside world. The white police run lucrative "protection" rackets in the ghetto in such illegal "businesses" as the numbers racket, bootlegging, prostitution, and extortion payments for not harassing Negroes who are engaged in legal enterprises. It is difficult, for instance, for a Negro to stay in the tavern or restaurant business in many areas of the South without paying off the cops so that they will not hang around the premises and intimidate the customers.

The fact that policemen in the South are largely recruited from the ranks of what is referred to as "poor white trash," the ignorant and the most embittered Negro-haters, is indicative of the true function of the southern police force. It is almost impossible for a Negro who grows up in the South to help from developing a condition-response of fear at the mere sight of a white man in a police uniform. As one Negro who is the son of a college president explained: "Man, when I see a cop I can't help but grow nervous and fearful inside even when I know I haven't done anything." This is so true that often when the Negro leaves the South and comes North, the same condition-response of fear persists at the sight of a cop on the street. Indeed, I myself have felt this fear, and, what is more, although I know better rationally, I cannot keep the adrenalin from shooting through my body when I see a policeman on the streets in New York City.

When a policeman is killed in the South, Negroes usually rejoice, no matter what the circumstances. The same emotions apply to what few Negro cops there are. In addition, the black cop is looked down upon by Negroes in a way which is at once pitiful and intensely hostile, because in fact the Negro cop in the South is only half a policeman. In most cases he can arrest only lawbreakers of his own race. If a white man breaks the law, the Negro cop must call a white officer to arrest the culprit. Because of this, the black cop usually hates himself so much that he takes it out on other Negroes with as much, if not more, brutality than his white counterpart. No matter what anybody says, I have come to believe that the one and only way to obliterate the Negro's predicament regarding the police is the absolute equal integration of the police, man for man, in proportion to the population statistics of blacks and whites, city by city, county by county, state by state.

Terror. More inordinate than hunger, the sense of violation has been the universal lot of all Negroes in the South. A terror so constant and ominous that the very metabolism of the people has been affected if not regulated by its tremor. The young as well as the old, the extremely dark as well as the light complexioned, the educated and well to do along with the ignorant and the poverty ridden, have all known the terror of personal intimidation, rape, murder, insult, blind hatred, human denial and outright assassination of individual character. Walking the streets, or sitting in his own living room, or asleep at night, no Negro can escape the sense that he has lived and is living in a terrorized region of the land where, of all things, the law itself is but a hollow name against the acting out, both concrete and subjective, of venom and hatred against his person, race and ethos.

Mississippi, Georgia, Alabama, South Carolina . . .

your mother, your father, your brothers, sisters, wives and daughters . . . spitfire of clubs, pistols, shotguns, the rope and the tree and the whip, the insults from children as well as from grown-ups, the missing, murdered, mutilated bodies of relatives and loved ones, curled out dead on the pavement, bodies blown to bits while praying for a better way of life in the House of the Lord, a torso sinking to the bottom of the lake . . . water hoses, electric prods, hound dogs, a thick shoe pounding the belly of a black woman sprawled in the Mississippi gravel beneath a signboard advertising sun lotion for the purity of the white race. The word, the symbol, the reality is *nigger*—and the reality is terror.

Dread. Out of the terror comes fear, a fear of danger against which one can do little or nothing. It is a fear that immobilizes the energies of the psyche—a hopelessness to which Negroes have had to adjust, if they were to retain any sanity at all. But how does one "adjust" to hopelessness? One posits in the world an omnipotent demon called "evil." Hopelessness becomes a *solemn state of mind*. Pain and anxiety provide no cessation of the *hurt* from *experiencing* pain and anxiety. One then can never in fact escape fear; one lives forever anticipating pain that he can do nothing about. The internalization of living in constant anticipatory fear of forces and conditions that are outraging one's life and against which one can do nothing—this is Dread. It is only recently that Negroes in the South, especially the young, have renounced this hopelessness and embarked upon a road to freedom. But the road is long and it is rugged, and dread will be a property of the Negro's life and consciousness until *all* the dangers and threats of the white world are wiped, absolutely, from the face of the Southland and the rest of this country.

Poverty. When we talk, with reference to the Negro, about equal job opportunity, fair employment, and so on, we are speaking about the lack of one thing. Money! The vast majority of southern Negroes have never been able to make enough money so that they can, at least in one area of their lives, experience the good life which is supposed to be peculiar to America. Poverty not only renders them physically derelict, but it also eats at their very personalities. The lack of money has deformed and is deforming the Negro's body, his sociophysical livelihood or existence, and his very mentality. The span of life plus the chances at life are limited and whittled away in direct proportion to the income of the southern Negro masses, which is far below that of most white people everywhere in America.

Death. Together, the ghetto, the police, terror, dread, and poverty, these forces and conditions in the South, constitute a crime immeasurably more hideous and inhuman than slavery or any other form of oppression. I am talking about genocide. To put it bluntly, not only has the Negro in the South been the constant victim of biological murder, but he has been the victim of both personal and institutionalized murder every day of his living life. By and large, despite the progress that is being made, all of the above conditions and forces still remain in the South today.

I feel the necessity to digress a moment. And yet, as you will see, what I have to say is not really a digression.

I have never heard anyone discuss the Jews in the South with reference to the Negro situation. Yet there are Jews in the South, and I know for a fact that their attitude and their behavior toward Negroes are noticeably different from those of whites in general. I am not referring to Jews such as, say, Harry Golden, and others of public note or national renown. On the contrary, I have in mind those thousands of Jews who may be spoken of as, and who are in fact, common or average people. To my mind, they constitute, with reference to the white South and the Negro, an enigma.

One of my first playmates was a Jew. We were both about five years old and the boy's family had a store in the heart of the black ghetto. I spent a great deal of my time in the store playing with the boy. Unlike my experience with other white boys, I do not recall his parents ever giving me or him the "eye" as a result of our getting too "close" or becoming too "intimate" in our friendship. At the time I did not know that they were Jews. I did know, however, that they were white.

Later, as I grew up, I worked a great deal for Jews, as delivery boy, handyman, and at other odd jobs. By my early teens I became conscious of these strange white people as being "Jews." I put the word in quotes because at that time the word did not mean anything to me except that they were whites who owned grocery and drygoods stores in Negro neighborhoods, and who owned pawn-shops and furniture stores and rented houses to black people. More important, however, at that time, the word "Jew" meant for me that these people treated Negroes far better than did any other whites, better even than the so-called "good" white folks. One was able to behave around them with far less apprehension. For a long time I was suspicious of these people because they were white and yet they behaved as if I might have been white my-self.

I remember the Jews in whose store I worked for a long time as delivery boy. Both the man and his wife treated me with unfeigned kindness, respect, and, as I have indicated, with an attitude that often frightened me. I was, for instance, always cringing away whenever the wife, moving around the store busy as hell, bumped unavoidably into me. When misunderstandings developed I found myself "talking back" to them and hearing them express authentic anger as if I were not colored or they were not white. In essence they treated me like a human being, and I in turn learned how to feel and act like one around them. Unlike the other whites, including the so-called "good" ones, I never heard or overheard them use the word "nigger," in reference to me or to any other Negro.

When I went away to college and first returned I went looking for the "Jew store." (That's what southern Negroes call neighborhood stores owned by Jews.) I spent an evening talking with them in their store, which had been moved across town to another black neighborhood. I remember they advised me to leave the South and never return. By this time I knew who and what Jews were. Since then I have wondered about the Jews in the South (not to mention those elsewhere).

Characteristically the Jews in the South earn a great deal of their livelihood from Negroes. In the ghetto the prevailing grocery store is the "Jew store." Many clothing and drygoods and furniture stores owned by Jews cater especially to Negroes. The same may be said of pawnshops, jewelry stores and loan companies. It seems that in the South, the North notwithstanding, but especially in the South the Jews, great numbers of them, earn their money in the Negro neighborhood, *but* they do not live there. This means that while they can and often do treat Negroes like human beings in their personal and commercial relations, they cannot or do not carry this behavior over into the social and political areas of life.

It is not difficult to understand why this is so. In the South, the Jews, like Negroes, are victims of prejudice and bigotry. Their places of worship, their homes and often their businesses are terrorized and even their very persons are frequently intimidated. This is specifically true if the Jews (or any one of them) should extend their humanity toward Negroes in ways that would be political or social. So while they are in a position somewhat similar to that of Negroes, they, for fear of reprisal from whites, stand aloof and watch the Negro suffer alone. And yet, when I think of what happened in Germany and Poland, I cannot help but wonder at the average Jew's aloofness from the Negro predicament in the South. It is not primarily because Jews are of white skin or because they own enterprises predominantly in Negro communities that they are victims of Negro anti-Semitism. Rather, it is because they have tended to exploit the Negro so long and have stood aloof from his political, social and economic plight in the South until they appear to many black people to be as hypocritical, if not as bigoted as the average white southern Protestant.

So I made a journey back to the Down-Home Country, back to the womb and the tomb, the birthplace of the living and the deathplace of the dying. I did not return with an ax to grind, I did not return to make trouble, neither did I go back with hate or bitterness. I went naked, with pathos in my heart and with a sure light in my mind. I came away with tears in my eyes, because, as I have stated, despite the changes for the better, I saw some things for the first time that caused me to worry and fear. And I severed the cords, all of them, with the South. I am at last free! Yet, because I am free, I hope that what follows here is mostly wrong.

Being and Blackness

Contrary to what we are accustomed to saying, especially those of us who consider ourselves in that mythical category of "liberals," the southern Negro—which means the majority of Negroes everywhere in this country—is not a man who "happens" to be a Negro. That's a lie. At best it is a semantic platitude. The American Negro is a man who *is* a Negro. This is to say that the black man is a Negro not by whimsy or chance or happenstance. Rather, he is a Negro by design, by purpose, by explicit cause. He is a Negro in part because he is *visible*, he is black. Because he is black he has historically been forced, and in large numbers still is forced, to be a "nigger." Because he is forced to be a Negro or a "nigger," he is *invisible* as a man or as a human being.

But black people in America are Negroes more than

with reference to their biology. Of course, I know, we all know, that without their biology, their blackness, the thing we call a "Negro" or a "nigger" would be impossible to cause or, if once caused, impossible to enforce. Blackness is a natural "uniform" that serves as convenient sociohuman clay which we mold into the subhuman species called the Negro. It is the *molding process* and the *ingredients* involved that are important. The ingredients that go to make up a Negro are of two classes, the objective and the subjective. Within the first class fall all of the concrete social, political, economic and human inequalities such as disenfranchisement, segregation, discrimination, lynching, and so on, to which black people have historically had and still have to submit. Any person of color who lives under these conditions in America is a Negro. But this constitutes only half of being Negro. Equally important is the kind of mentality toward himself and the world that develops in the psyche of a person who lives under such conditions. Along with the objective conditions that constitute being a Negro, there is a distinct psychology, a definite personality structure that characterizes the Negro and sets him aloof from all other Americans, even Puerto Ricans. None of this is accidental.

Furthermore, none of this is inherited, none of it is biological in source. My own son, for instance, who at the time was no more than three or four years old, spent several months down South. When he returned to New York, I noticed a definite change in his personality development with reference to himself, to other black people, and to "white folks." Before he left New York people were people, and he liked or disliked them on a basis other than their color. However, when he returned, he remarked rather derogatorily about a friend whom he had liked very much. "William is *black*, ain't he?" And at a white friend whom he had also liked he just stood and stared in a sort of withdrawn and puzzled manner. I observed also that whenever he saw colored people on television, he pointed at them, he laughed or grew quiet, but always with discernible anxiety. Before my son went South people were people and he was merely a little boy. When he returned, people were no longer people, his personality was no longer developing as a little boy but as a *Negro* boy. Later, when I heard him use the word "nigger," I knew (oh yes, I knew) that forces of racism in America were well under way, crippling my son, alienating him from the human race and, above all, from himself.

That the Negro's consciousness, especially in the South, is *totalitarianized* by racist values that compel him to hate himself, to act and think like, and in fact to be a Negro, is no exaggeration. Understand that to be born black or colored does not automatically, in the sense of which I am speaking, make one a "Negro." A "Negro" is not only an inferior human status in our society, it is the reflection of and the negative valuation of this derogatory human status in the behavior and the mind of colored people toward the world and, most of all, toward themselves. Psychologically, to be a "Negro" is to be a specific personality configuration, the elements of which consist of various and varying forms of self, that is Negro, depreciation. Accordingly, the colored child learns to be a "Negro" not only because of direct experience of the white world's hatred—he also learns to be Negro from other Negroes. The few months my son was down South, he did not have much, if any, contact with bigoted whites. He lived with and moved among other Negroes, predominantly his own relatives.

It is no wonder to me now that when I was trying to be an actor, some Negroes, thrilled over my performances, would almost invariably "compliment" me, *not* by saying what a fine actor I could become, but by telling me what a great preacher I could be. I recall that in the South when a colored person projected an outlook toward himself and the world that was not depreciatory, other Negroes would often remark, "That nigger thinks he's white." Moreover, and this is very important in learning to be a "Negro," being Negro means that one becomes neurotically involved with one's *mouth, hair,* and *shade* of color. As a boy I was slapped on my mouth on many occasions simply because I forgot to hold it

39

pressed tightly. My people did not want me to develop "thick" lips. Extremely dark Negroes, men and women, are considered attractive only if their features approach Caucasian ones (that is, thin straight hair—"good" hair, keen noses and unpronounced cheek bones). Such Negroes are not referred to as being black *and* beautiful, rather as being black BUT beautiful.

I have written elsewhere that blackness is conceived in the Negro personality as a sort of mystical *iniquity* of his *being*. I am not merely referring to those Negroes who are very dark. The objective subhuman status of the Negro in the racist world, plus the Negro's own depreciatory preoccupation with his features and his lower status, dominates and structures, in predominantly *all* American people of color—rich, poor, light, dark— that however well-guarded, self-conscious, self-loathing psyche configuration known as the "American Negro." A psyche source alienated from believing in its own validity! Or if the Negro "loves" himself, rather than genuine self-appreciation, it is more often than not a pathological attempt to counteract his and the white world's derogatory valuation of the Negro as a character structure "different" from that of whites. This animal, this creature we have forced and molded into the derogatory thing we call "Negro" will be with us until the last vestiges of racism are utterly demolished. It has not been the black people who have created their own social and psychological degradation. It has been the morality of the white world which has alienated black people from the beauty and the dignity of their blackness, their *ethos,* from life, liberty, and the pursuit of happiness.

The Existential Negroes

When it comes to self-appreciation, to life, liberty and the pursuit of happiness, the most abandoned people in America are the black southern masses. Those Negroes we refer to as dirty, as drunkards, the lazy and the boisterous; those who are uneducated, "uncultured"; those black men and women who clean our houses, who dig our ditches, scrub our toilets, sweat and toil in our foundries, dispose of our garbage, cook our food and wash the dirty dishes; those who hang out on the corners of the ghetto and "hustle" for a living, the gamblers, thieves, whores, dope addicts; those who have renounced religion because they feel that there is no God; and those who wring themselves to conniptions on the wooden or marble floors of sacred escape from secular desolation because they, too, know there is no salvation on this earth; all of these black people are forced by us, and us alone, to live their lives in a most despicable state of wretchedness. No argument that you or I might conjure up can excuse this democracy for its almost total neglect and exploitation of the black masses who constitute more than 90 per cent of all Negroes in our republic. Somewhere in our minds, in our emotions, we all know very well that within the realm of the kind of political, economic, and social system we call the "American Democracy," it is impossible for the bulk of Negroes ever to achieve anything that approaches an equality with the rest of us. Indeed, even when we are saying so, we seldom really want it to happen.

Therefore we hate the masses because their wretchedness reminds us of our gainsay. We neglect, exploit, and abandon them because it is our purpose, the very function of our way of life, to neglect, exploit, and degrade them. This equally applies to the few Negroes in this country who are "making it." Those who are middle class and those who are merely middle class *oriented* have the same disposition toward the black masses as whites do. When the Negro "leaders" rally the masses into a half-closed fist or a bureaucratic and dangerous parade against the "ills" of this democracy, their plans and aspirations *rarely* include anything that will *in fact* erase the economic, political, and personal horror from the lives of the Negro masses. No matter what is proclaimed by the "leaders," most of what is achieved, or all that their programs will lead to, is a better chance for those who are "qualified" to climb the American ladder of success. Of course, "qualified" means conforming to the very system which, if the masses are to be free, must be destroyed.

The Negro masses in the South have been, still are, and no doubt will continue to be deprived of access to any of the significant institutions, within their own race as well as without, in and through which they can acquire that *dignity of self* without which the human animal is no more than a wretch of alien forces. The masses have been and are, in the sense I am speaking, neglected by their own race. When desegregation, and all the rest come, there is little reason to suppose that they will be any better off. To wit, the ideology, or the morality, of those institutions that Negroes are seeking to desegregate will continue to exclude the bulk of the black masses, because the morality and the structure of these institutions—schools, political office, the military, business, and even the ballot—will still be determined by a specific group of people who adhere to a philosophy which defines the characteristic way men stand in relation to property, work, technology, money, and the distribution of national wealth. An economic, sociopolitical mode and philosophy which make it possible for only a few people to gain or even *aspire* to gain access to those institutions that lead to the so-called "good life," this kind of mode and this kind of philosophy will *not* be destroyed, barring world catastrophe, or "overthrown," but will run the gamut of their more or less natural and painful history.

So the masses of black people in the South, along with most of those in northern ghettos, are the existential rot of our nation. When I say "existential rot," I am not making a value judgment (whatever that is), nor am I being poetic. Rather, I am talking about the objective phenomena, both physical and sociopsychological, that characterize the *existence* of the black masses. There is, for instance, a tendency for whites and blacks to think of lower-class Negroes as "scum," as "hoodlums."

During the rioting that shook many of the northern ghettos in the summer of 1964, the press, whites in responsible positions, and the general populace asserted that the rioters were predominantly from the "hoodlum element" of the Negro communities in question. Immediately after the riots, I took an interviewing position with one of the largest research organizations in this country. One of the things asked of the people in the riot areas (Harlem and Bedford Stuyvesant) was what "types" of persons did they think participated in the riots. Almost invariably the contemptuous response from these Negroes was, "riffraff, dope addicts, hoodlums. . . ." These responses came from older Negroes who were or who thought of themselves as "cultured and middle class."

On the other hand, when I talked to many of the younger Negroes who admitted their part in the rioting, I found them to be something other than mere derelicts. Several were college students on vacation, and while a

44

few stated that the riots might have included some derelicts motivated by a desire for pillage, almost all of them denied that the riots were caused entirely by this element. In fact, the younger Negroes were more knowledgeable, analytical, and more realistic regarding their interpretation of and participation in the riots than most of the older Negroes. A great many of the older Negroes exhibited middle-class attitudes of shame and offered clichés and stereotyped explanations in discussing the riots.

I am reminded of a youth, probably about fourteen or fifteen years of age, who, during the zenith of the rioting in Harlem, fell in with my pace as I hurried up 128th Street toward Seventh Avenue, where the police were being bombarded with bottles, bricks, beer cans, and other debris. The youth took one glance at me and immediately recognized that I was not from Harlem (they can do that, you know). He thought I was a reporter. I told him that I was a poet and a writer, and that I was concerned about what was going on. As if he were an expert (which he probably was), he began telling me what "perpetrated" the rioting. In summing up, he said he had a "theory" about the terror that existed in Harlem. I was amazed at his language, at his intelligence, at his general countenance. He told me that he was a George Washington High School student and was majoring in business education. Then, to my surprise,

I saw he had a Pepsi-Cola bottle and, before I could say anything, he hurled it over the heads of hundreds of rioting Negroes smack into the chalk face of a white helmet!

My point is this. If the Negroes who were rioting in Harlem, Brooklyn, and other areas were predominantly "hoodlums," then at least 90 per cent of all Negroes in the United States are "hoodlums." Not only has America deprived the bulk of her Negroes, she has *depraved* them. America has forced them to live and think as if they were less than human. Why was that youth, who was obviously intelligent and ambitious, and who should have been in his home studying or somewhere engaged in more fruitful behavior, out there flinging bottles at the police? Why were they all there? I will tell you why. Because they, along with their parents and their peers, have been and are abandoned by America to rats and roaches that infest the wretched tenements of high rental slum lords. They have been abandoned by America to the dope gangsters (not merely the pushers!) and dope politicians; to individual and collective attitudes and acts of rejection as well as psychological and bodily mutilation; to crooked finance companies, pawnshops, dishonest merchants, police brutality; and finally to disease, hopelessness, and ultimately to death.

Down South I walked the ghetto hovels of these wretched and forlorn multitudes. In the "Negro section" of every southern town, on the "main drags," in liquor joints and beer joints, in poolrooms, barbershops, in dingy luncheonettes, everywhere, the black masses are the lowly and the lonely. They are the cultural alienates, the *wretched elite*. Unlike the professional and skilled Negroes, the southern black masses consisting of domestics, unskilled laborers, hustlers, and the unemployed, all are without hope of ever achieving a better life. Or if they have hope, it is a fool's hope in which the American Dream is but the shining chrome of an automobile for which they will forever owe another part of their lives to another white man. For the black masses never have enough money. They possess no land and there is little chance of their ever acquiring any. They have nothing to claim or reclaim. Deep in the recesses of their psyches they are aware that the "Negro Revolution" is not, when it comes to them, really a revolution. They are totally demilitarized. Although they have fought and died in many foreign lands and jungles, in the jungles of their own country they cannot even defend themselves when "white folks" are spitting on them, setting dogs on them, throwing bricks and riding horses on them, and prodding them with cattle rods and kicking them and calling them niggers and killing them.

They are the existential Negroes. They have no art except their gut-bucket songs which are embezzled, vulgarized, and turned into alien commodities by white misfits here and abroad. No one has ever written *about* them except Richard Wright, and he was hounded out of the South, hounded out of the country. No one has ever written *for* them except Langston Hughes, and he is branded a "dirty commie" and threatened every time he goes down there. They have no artifacts except a treacherous symbol on the walls of their shanties, a symbol that "white folks" have repeatedly burnt to ash and bone in the dirt of their front yards.

Yet, over the decades, it has been their muscles that have hewn out the ditches. Their black hands have handled the molten steel. Their black bodies have glistened in the southern sun like the hot tar they poured on the streets and highways, often with chains around their ankles. Their musty sweat has coagulated with the dust and dirt on the concrete floors of the foundries and factories. Their brute labor has picked and shoveled the coal out of the mountains. They have lost their lives on the dams and bridges. The soil itself has been fertilized with their bodies and the running of their tears. Their backbones have mixed and lifted the mortar and bricks that raised the buildings. Their agile fingers have been whittled away, planting and picking the cotton, fruit, and the vegetation. Alas, their succulent breasts and soft thighs have nursed and nurtured not only their men and the children of their men, but

48

the very sons and daughters of the men who have violated their bodies and their persons for centuries.

You! You tell these people that they are not entitled
to anything equal with you in this great country, that
they are not worthy of full-fledged citizenship, and that
their personality, their ethos, is not a composite product
of the American experience, and therefore somehow is
not as *valid* as "your" personality and "your" ethos!

It smacks of madness. And this madness, this absur-
dity, is driving the Negro mad as certainly as you are
mad. So far, however, you have forced the Negro, the
existential Negro, to contain *your* madness within himself, within the suppressed rage and white heat of the
black ghetto. And he has had to act it all out within and
upon himself. He, the Negro of the masses, especially
in the South, has been forced to believe and, in fact, to
know that he is, after all, the dark counterpart of *your*
iniquity, "a nigger."

He, the existential Negro, is not in a quandary about
his "identity." That quandary is the trap of Negroes
who have taken in the mores and the intellectualisms
of the white world without having been fully accepted
by that world. That quandary is the trap of those Negroes
who ride, so to speak, on the rim or margin of two
worlds, the black world and the white world—Baldwin,
Ellison, Dr. DuBois, and perhaps myself even. This is
not so with the black man in the masses. He wears a

mask because the white world has forced it, like a skin, upon him. His mask is his condition and the personality determined from and by that condition. America, the South in particular, has stripped him of almost everything good in himself as a human being except his terrible spontaneity. And America has vested in *him* the awful monster of what racism in this country has done not merely to the Negro's humanity but to the white's as well. But, as history will bear me out, the time will come (it is already coming) when all the demons we have vested in the Negro will *explode,* like brimstone, hail and fire, up and down the land. When this happens, finally, I trust we will be able to live and work together like men. Because then there will be no other way, save death for us all.

1965
New York

ANOTHER MAN DONE GONE

CHAPTER 2

AND YOU, TOO, SIDNEY POITIER!

I remember the first time I went to the movies, or as they called it in those days, the "picture show." One Friday my stepfather and my mother took my younger brother and me down the main street in the Negro section of Chattanooga, Tennessee, past pawnshops and liquor stores, poolrooms and beer joints, past hordes of swarthy Negroes leaning on corners and thronging the littered pavement, to where a long line of colored folks stood outside a great crumbling structure with neon signs flashing on and off. Inside, on the screen, a young beautiful woman, dressed in the most elegant gown, who looked like she was not of the colored race, sang "tick-a-tock-tick-a-tock." Another young woman, very brown and somehow motherly looking, cried and sang softly as she hugged a man's shirt while it hung drying on the wash-line. A very handsome light-skinned man with long straight black hair, wearing a very loose-fitting suit, pranced and glided across the screen while his hair flopped about his head and face, singing "hi-di-hi-di-ho!"

I learned later that one woman was Lena Horne, the other, Ethel Waters, and the man, the indomitable and flamboyant Cab Calloway. They were Negro personalities that down-South colored folks could be and indeed were proud of. It was all so thrilling. But, somehow, some way, even as a child who knew nothing about acting, I felt that something was lacking in their performance. Despite their great singing and dancing and cooing, and definitely despite their prettiness, they did not strike me as being as *real* in what they were doing as, say, the Negroes I had passed that evening on the street. Although I had enjoyed what I had seen, I was left a little confused.

From that time on I made a point of seeing films in which there were Negroes. Eventually I learned the names of the more prominent film personalities: Ralph Cooper, Herb Jeffries, Mantan Moreland, Stepin Fetchit, Canada Lee, Juan Hernandez, Rochester, Bo-jangles, Noble Sissle, and the rest. All of them entertained me greatly. In fact, that's all most of them were, entertainers. By this I mean they were either clowns and buffoons with big rolling eyes and invariably afraid of haunted houses, or they were maids and butlers and musicians and singers and tap dancers and band leaders. The few who did not conform to the above stereotypes were poor mimics of white gangsters (Ralph Cooper) and white cowboys (Herb Jeffries); or they struck me as "foreign" black men with strange accents (Hernandez and Lee) who had never lived in America, at least not in the America I knew.

By this time I was fully aware of what had perplexed me as a small boy that day my mother had taken me to see *Stormy Weather*. There had been too much artificiality. It was the absence of the *reality* of Negroes as men and the absence of the *reality* of Negroes as *dramatic* individuals, as I knew them to be in everyday life. In too many instances, it was the negation of the Negro's very humanity in terms of the authentic portrayal of his personality as an entire integrity rather than a fractionary dysfunction. The integrated complexity of the Negro's personality never came to bear upon any one or a variety of situations. Only singular aspects of the Negro—his dancing, or musical, comic, religious, bellicose, or sly characteristics, to name a few—were portrayed, as if they represented the whole of his emotional wellspring.

The first film I saw in which the Negro did not appear as a complete- or semi-caricature was *Home of the Brave*, starring James Edwards. At that time the name of James Edwards was unknown and until his appearance I had begun to grow fearful that perhaps Negroes really did lack the capacity for dramatic portrayal. It was as if they had a deep psychological block, stemming from their racial experiences, that prevented them from performing as straight human beings rather than as mere entertainers. But my fear was dispelled or at least mitigated when I saw James Edwards play the role of a Negro soldier in foreign combat who not only became a hero because of his bravery against the enemy, but who also showed manly prowess in regard to the prejudice of his white comrades. James Edwards was not the best actor I had dreamed of. He was a little too stiff and somewhat slow on cues. Yet he played a proud role in which not merely one but many aspects of his personality (as a *human being* who was a Negro) came through. To me this was a definite sign that Negroes were not necessarily inferior performers. It gave me hope that one day, if Negroes fought diligently, America would have to let black men appear on the screen like bonafide actors with complete integrity regarding their humanity and the essential realism of the situations they might portray.

As is evident now, my hope was not without some degree of realization. There is at least one Negro who has pounced on the American screen and, like a jet, has soared to fame and stardom. What is important here is that Sidney Poitier is not an entertainer, not a singer or a comedian or a musician. Rather, he is strictly an *actor*.

When I first saw him on the screen I was shocked,

dumbfounded and delighted. I believe it was around 1955, and Poitier starred in a television drama called *A Man Is Ten Feet Tall*. The story was about a Negro dock worker, a foreman as a matter of fact, who befriends a timid and very insecure white worker against the brutes and roughnecks of the dock, and especially against the southern-born, racist head foreman. The head foreman, of course, hates Poitier because of his color. Moreover, he hates him for his manly attitude in that Poitier does not play the usual role of "Uncle Tom." Envying the friendship between Poitier and the timid white worker, the head foreman proceeds to take out his venom on the white worker whom Poitier defends, ultimately, by way of a hook duel in which the foreman unfairly kills Poitier. In the end the timid worker gains courage and avenges Poitier's death first by beating the foreman, and then by breaking the "silent code" of the docks and literally dragging the murderer to the authorities. The play was later made into a movie entitled *Edge of the City*.

Since that movie Poitier has played, always with great skill and dignity, a variety of starring roles, so that he has become, by all standards, one of America's best actors. His winning of the Academy Award indubitably marked a historic occasion in the annals of Hollywood. What is important about all this is not so much that a Negro has finally won an Academy Award—not this alone; rather, it is the fact that Hollywood and the general public (both white and black) have accepted the *kind* of Negro that Poitier characteristically portrays on the screen. First of all, he is *all* Negro. He is black, his features are markedly Negroid, his body is long and regal, his hands are large and dexterous, his hair is rather "nappy," and he has thick, agile lips. In combination these features make Poitier an unusually powerful figure on the screen. Secondly, his style of acting has involved the entire range of Negro behavior and personality characteristics vehicled by what is known as the "method" technique. Invariably, his role interpretations are rugged, bold, and without the slightest suggestion of "Uncle Tomism," which is to say that everything about his projections definitely lets one know Poitier is authentically Negro. He is no caricature, no stereotyped colored man acting out one or several fractionalized aspects of the Negro personality which whites usually demand of black actors.

For instance, in *Edge of the City* we see Poitier as a laborer, a philosopher, a family man, a friend of the underdog, a dreamer, a man of sensibility, and as a person of courage and dignity. These qualities are projected as only a man who has experienced what it is to be a Negro in America can project them. In other words, with reference to "method" acting, Poitier has what, among others, Paul Newman and Rod Steiger have, plus the added ingredient of his *Negritude*. As a Negro, this makes him more convincing than, say, Belafonte or James Edwards, or even Ossie Davis. In fact, Belafonte and Edwards have something about them that smacks of the nice middle-class Negro; and Ossie Davis reminds one of the old, stereotyped Harlem Theatre Guild Negro actor with the booming voice of a pork chop preacher but without much finesse or genius. Perhaps the only other Negro actor who can rival Poitier in terms of power, genius, and the ability to project himself as an authentic and total human force, is William Marshall. But Marshall is so powerful an actor, in physical stature as well as in role projection, that Hollywood, with the exception of playing him as some kind of warrior or gladiator, simply does not know what to do with him. So Marshall is doing much better in Europe where the fear of the authentic Negro is not so much a part of the European cultural dread, and Poitier is more or less left alone to bear the entire burden and glory of portraying the Negro in America as a true and integral human force.

Even when Poitier plays a role such as the one he played in "Something of Value," where he must be somewhat subservient, it is somehow done with dignity and the full impact of a total, however obsequious, human being—in glaring contrast to, say, Archie Moore's stereotyped, lopsided, artificial portrayal of an Uncle-Tom-type

Negro in *The Carpetbaggers,* or *Huckleberry Finn.* Of
course, Archie Moore is no actor. And it is revealing why
Hollywood would choose him and others like him to play
such roles as he has been playing. There is nothing
wrong with the Negro being portrayed as an Uncle Tom
or as any other derogatory generalization, *so long as the
human quality of the characterization comes through.*
There is rarely anything artificial and dehumanized about
Poitier, neither in his performances as they relate to the
art of acting nor as they relate to the human reality of
the Negro. This is what makes Poitier great. In all that
he does, he does himself justice as an actor and does
the Negro justice as a human being, except in one
regard. This exception is perhaps the most crucial and
sensitive area of our lives.

I have stated that the thing that troubled me about
most Negroes in movies was that they, for all of their
entertainment value, never seemed real in what they
were doing in comparison to the way they are in actual
life. I said, something was missing. Sidney Poitier does
seem, at first scrutiny, very much real. Yet, when one
probes deeply into all the films in which he has played,
for every coefficient of Negro life as that life is lived
in the real world, one discovers something frightening
and terrible. There is something systematically missing,
the absence of which turns Poitier, no matter how brilliantly he performs, into a caricature of the Negro that

is as artificial and dehumanizing, if not more so, as all
the other Hollywood vulgar negations of the black man
as a complex, integral human being.

I am talking about the absence, in *all* the Poitier movies,
of the primeval emotion, and of that deep psyche-physical
yearning to mate with the opposite sex. Why can't Sidney
Poitier, since he is such a superb actor, make love in the
movies?

No amount of argument can convince me that Poitier
is incapable of effectively portraying an amorous involvement on the screen. Neither is it reasonable to say that
Poitier is the wrong "type" to make love in the movies.
After all, as I have pointed out, Poitier and Paul Newman
are the same type of actors, and Newman makes love
on the screen constantly. Newman is white. And now
we are getting close to the problem—Poitier's blackness,
his "Negroness."

The fact that Poitier cannot or does not make love in
the movies is a manifestation of American racism as it
relates to the sexuality of the Negro. Elsewhere I have
written that by and large white America conceives of
the Negro as sexually vulgar and repulsive; to see a
Negro kiss or pet on the screen would send large numbers
of white people, throughout the United States, cringing
and recoiling in prurient disgust or excitement. It would
be too much for the sexual insecurity and anxiety that
the majority of American whites have, not only about

the Negro, but about themselves as well. Therefore, the black man in mass media, the cinema especially, must be desexed. And by desexing the Negro, America is denying him his manhood, which ultimately means the negation of his very humanity. This is precisely what Hollywood has done and is doing to, ironically (or is it quite naturally?), the only Negro who has won an Academy Award.

Sidney Poitier and Paul Newman, along with Diahann Carroll and Joanne Woodward, were the stars in a movie called *Paris Blues*. As the story goes, Poitier and Newman are jazz musicians in Paris. One night, after their performance they meet a couple of girls outside the supper club. The two couples confront each other and Diahann Carroll, the colored girl, seems to be fascinated by Paul Newman. For a quick moment it appears as if the foursome is going to pair off interracially. Suddenly Miss Carroll, as if something snaps in her or, better yet, as if on cue from the director, rejects Newman and comes on to her black brother, Poitier.

While there are numerous scenes showing Newman and Miss Woodward hugging, petting, kissing, and even lying around in bed together, there are "equivalent" scenes of Poitier and Miss Carroll walking around Paris, stopping here and there, taking in the sights, and *discussing the race problem*. At one "high" point Poitier *actually* gets a chance to touch Miss Carroll's hand. That's all, brother, that's all.

What is so false and artificial about the entire story is that Poitier, a jazz musician, gets involved, no, gets *associated* with a middle-class, nice-nice, sexually rigid Negro woman who is hung-up about living up to some kind of "race pride." And she convinces Poitier to come back "home" and be a "shining knight" for his people. What a joke! Everybody knows, and I do mean everybody, including Hollywood and the NAACP, that no jazz musician is *that* "nice." There are plenty of Negro women like the one portrayed by Miss Carroll, but you will seldom, if ever, find a jazz musician giving one of them a second thought. Yet I know, we all know, why the pairing-off did not happen interracially. It probably would have caused a riot on Broadway and a slaughter in Alabama. In essence, by denying Poitier the right to make love with either of the women, Hollywood endeavored to play up to the fears of white America, on the one hand, and make the Negro "presentable" to black people, on the other. On both accounts they succeeded only in telling the public a lie. And, incidentally, the movie was the lousiest Poitier film I have seen.

In *The Long Ships* Poitier plays a dashing Moorish prince with not only a beautiful wife but an entire pavilion of pretty girls. He is respected throughout his kingdom. He fights well, and people bow down in his presence. He is the dashing black prince! But for all of that, he is more interested in some golden bell than he is in his most attractive and love-starved wife. In one scene the wife actually begs him and pulls on his arm (nothing else) to stay with her, to give her some of his affection. The black prince stands there rigid like a eunuch; he pushes her aside and runs off looking for gold.

On the other hand, Richard Widmark comes from another land and runs amuck with the women of Poitier's court. Widmark, a white man, ultimately seduces the very wife of the black prince, while the black prince is sitting in a tent talking "intrigue" with Widmark's wife.

All of this is so telling. The sexual stereotypes of black and white are completely reversed: the Negro is "impotent," the white man is "virile." It is not beyond imagination that there might have been some Moorish kings who were homosexuals or "faggots," or what have you. But why did Hollywood have to make such a *point* of this? Why, for instance, did they not put less stress on this aspect, or omit it altogether? I assert that it was no accident. While it may not have been consciously deliberate, it represents a pattern, a systematic attempt to castrate Sidney Poitier in the movies. This signifies, insofar as Poitier in the movies must be a symbolic representation of America's concept of the Negro in general, the outright denial of manhood with reference to all black Americans.

The most "immaculate" version of the desexing of Poitier as an actor is, of course, the role which won him the Academy Award. To me *Lilies of the Field* is a pitiful joke. Picture this—here is a tall, regal, young black man in tight white pants that reveal his every muscle, jumping and running around with a group of nuns. (Incidentally, they are foreigners.) He even shows his naked bulging chest. He is *sexy*, nobody can deny that. One need not belabor the twisted psychological subtleties of this movie. Yet I am compelled to point out that white America can let its imagination run wild, secure in the knowledge that nothing can really happen between that sexy black boy and those white nuns.

No doubt, it appears as if I am being unduly critical about all of this. I don't think so. To illustrate further, let's take a movie (or several movies) where there is some amount of affection between a Negro and a woman. I have in mind *The World, the Flesh, and the Devil* in which Harry Belafonte and a white woman find themselves the only two people left on earth after a strange, presumably nuclear catastrophe. After a great deal of beating around the bush, so to speak, it comes out that the two are definitely interested in each other. There is one scene in which Belafonte cuts the woman's hair—a fine symbolic rite. Although the movie smacks of reality (that is, within the limits of the situation), and is a fine piece of filming and story plotting, the feigned affection between Belafonte and the woman is never realized because a third man pops up, a white man. You know what happens then. Nevertheless the story held together all the way through to the end (mainly because of the skillful plotting) where the woman stops the two men from fighting and takes both the white man's hand and Belafonte's, and leads them off to what can be taken for, under the circumstances, a "brighter horizon."

Although *The World, the Flesh, and the Devil* is the best Hollywood film of its kind, I must point out several things about it that I consider important. First of all, throughout the entire movie the woman is the aggressor, which strikes me as unlikely, or at best, seems like a "neat trick." Secondly, Harry Belafonte is a light-skinned Negro; and granted that if a nuclear situation such as this were to happen, it seems statistically improbable, to say the least, that the one Negro to survive would be a light-skinned, sexually timid type with a morality which comes close to that reputed to be of the respectable white middle class. Especially, since Belafonte's occupation in the movie was as a coal miner and a crack electrician.

Let us examine an extreme example of, for want of a better term, "whitewashing" or "Caucasianizing" the Negro in films that deal with or purport to deal with interracial love. The film is *One Potato, Two Potato*, which was praised by most of the critics (of course, the critics are white). As the story goes, there is this lonely and single Negro living in a small northern town. One day he meets this white divorcée at a picnic. As time goes on they keep running into each other and consequently start dating which leads, after a while, to their getting married. Of course, the woman abandons her friends and the Negro's parents do not accept their white daughter-in-law until she gives birth to a mulatto baby.

Bernie Hamilton (the Negro) did a magnificent job of "acting." I have known him personally for years and I barely recognized him. Although he is an extremely handsome, masculine, dynamic, and rugged type of Negro, in that film he was so middle-class, so sissyfied, so desexed that his metamorphosis would have shocked Kafka. He kissed the white woman once, and it was so artificial, so plastic (that's the word, *plastic*) that one wondered why did they bother at all.

The second factor is the woman's first child (a girl) and the white deserter father. One day he turns up looking for his daughter, now that he has "gotten religion" and wants to fulfill his fatherly responsibilities. Racial-sex rage explodes within him when he finds that his former wife and daughter are living with Negroes. Now this man is a "liberal," and he knows (no doubt in his "heart") that he is wrong. Nevertheless he succumbs right there on the wide screen to all the pathological emotions that racists feel about Negro men and white women.

67

He institutes a law suit to gain custody of his daughter, whom he deserted years ago, on the basis of an "unfit" home. The judge in the suit, who is also no doubt a "liberal," admits that the father is wrong. Nevertheless, he takes the child from the people she has come to love and gives her to the deserter father. Pitifully he rationalizes his decision on the "basis" of "what's going to happen to this little white girl when she grows up if she continues to live with Negroes." The thing I want to know is why, if they really wanted to make an honest movie, didn't the moviemakers (who I am sure conceived of their efforts as "liberal") employ some *positive* gimmicks instead of all of the negative ones? The child, for instance, did not have to be a girl, it could have been a boy, and the judge would not have had to worry about the eventual "pollution" of the chastity of a "darling lily."

Finally—and this is the worst cop-out—while Bernie Hamilton is extremely handsome, the white woman's physical appearance does not match his by any stretch of the imagination. This observation is not intended as a personal slander against Barbara Barrie, who is a fine actress and I would imagine, from the human pathos that shines through her face, a very wonderful person. The fact remains, however, that Miss Barrie looked extremely drab, unattractive, and plain in that movie. This satisfies the stereotype that *any* kind of white woman will do for

68

a Negro, and of any kind it is the most unattractive types that will marry "one." If the moviemakers had any desire to be true to what they pretended to be undertaking, why, since at least Bernie Hamilton is so attractive, did they not employ an actress who equaled or surpassed him in physical qualities? Contrary to the reviewers, *One Potato, Two Potato* is a supreme example of subterranean confirmation of the prejudices, anxieties, and fears that out-and-out racists entertain toward love across the color line. It is the double-talking that characterizes too many would-be white liberals.

But why talk only about racists and so-called white liberals? Negroes tend to adhere to the same systematic mode of desexing themselves in the cinema just as whites do and just as the American public seems bent on demanding. Of course, Negroes who do not adhere to the practice of sterilizing themselves in the visual arts are apt to find that their works will lie around unproduced, or, if produced, will be killed at the box office. But when a few Negroes who have independent means still conform to the same protocol as do the white writers and producers, it means that Negroes have sufficiently internalized the racist concept of, among other things, their sexuality and therefore are ashamed of their nature, and are participating in the denial of one of the bases of their very humanity.

Sidney Poitier does not have the opportunity to act out

love emotions even in an all-Negro movie, because, as it were, the Negro author (the late Lorraine Hansberry) of *A Raisin in the Sun* did not choose to emphasize love and tenderness between men and women as vital aspects of Negro life. And where these aspects are brought up in other all-Negro movies, such as in *The Cool World* and *Nothing but a Man*, the treatment of them is so skimpy and glossed over that one gets the impression that if the moviemakers were to treat sexual emotions of and between black people in America in an authentic and human fashion, all hell would break loose. No doubt it would.

To recognize the *human validity* of Negro sexuality is one of the necessary ways of affirming the Negro's essential manhood. This would constitute a tumultuous psychological revolution with ramifications no less significant than the changes resulting from current civil rights activities.

CHAPTER 3

GRAMMAR OF THE NEGRO REVOLUTION

ILLUSION AND REALITY

Contrary to the way we are accustomed to thinking, the race problem is not a "freak" condition in our midst. It is a natural phenomenon, logical and predictable. Similar to the existence of organized crime and the problems surrounding it, the Negro's condition in our society and the problems surrounding this condition have tended to be, and still tend to be, *an ongoing American institution*. The significance of this point of view is that it necessitates a change in our thinking about the cause of and the persistence of the race problem, thereby forcing us to change our thinking about how to get rid of it, if we really want to, or better still, if we can *afford* to.

The major function of any institution is to maintain and promote the very kind of political, economic, and social relations in and out of which the institution arises. If an institution is or becomes totally incongruous to a society or a nation, the nation or society will either drive the institution underground or wipe it out completely. A clear example of this is the institution of slavery. When, as one form of Negro oppression, slavery became totally disastrous to the continued growth and development of industrial capitalism and its complex political and social functions, the nation rose up *in arms* and stamped slavery out. But the nation has not seen fit to rise up in arms, or in much of any other way, to wipe out that form of Negro oppression which succeeded slavery. This is because the modern form of oppression, known as segregation and discrimination, is part and parcel of the institutional necessities that lend dynamics to "our kind of society." The so-called race problem has logically emerged, or has been created, out of the total historical complex of our lives. This complex which is also social, economic, and political has given rise to, and still gives rise to, Negro oppression as an *institution* in the fabric of our nation. This institution is at once inimical to the *morality* of the "Democratic Creed" and basic to the *practicality* of the American Establishment (the Nation State), as that Establishment has *objectively* existed in the past and as it exists today.

I am not implying that the American sociopolitical-capitalistic complex which includes, among other things, the way men stand in relationship to money, to property and to capital equipment, the basis upon which goods and services are distributed, and, most of all, the way men stand in relationship to other men (*power*)—I am not saying that this complex is the *cause* of the oppressive condition of the American Negroes. What I am asserting is that the existence and continuation of the current form (as well as all future forms) of Negro oppression is a logically functioning part of the sociopolitical-capitalistic machinery that propels this nation in the way it has been going, is going, and will go. Hardly anybody, especially among Negroes, when speaking of the "dynamics" which make America a great nation, realizes that the Negro's status as an underdog is definitely one of those "dynamics." Specifically, because of the total interconnectedness of every aspect of American life, the Negro, in gaining his complete freedom, will discover that many of the things he has fought for will no longer be available, that is, within the economic-political framework that characterizes this nation.

The persistence of Negro oppression, in one form or another, largely derives from the way Negroes as well as whites have conceptualized or misconceptualized the entire problem of race relations in America. This is especially true when it comes to the so-called "Negro Revolution."

The history of the Negro's struggle to overcome op-

73

pression reads like the history of the American political
economy itself. Putting it roughly, it goes something like
this: the rise of the abolitionist movement . . . pairing
off of North vs. South . . . the war . . . the abolition of
slavery . . . the Reconstruction period . . . establishment of the Freedmen's bureau . . . the Compromise of
1876 . . . withdrawal of northern troops from the South
. . . disbandment of the Freedmen's bureau . . . rise of
the KKK . . . riots, lynchings . . . new disenfranchisement of Negroes . . . emergence of peon cropping system in the South . . . rise of Jim Crow, segregation, discrimination . . . Booker T. Washington, "separate like
the fingers" . . . the Atlanta Compromise . . . split in
Negro leadership: W. E. B. Dubois vs. Booker T.
Washington . . . the founding of the NAACP . . .
World War I . . . migration of Negroes to the North
. . . Scottsboro boys . . . World War II . . . desegregation of Armed Forces . . . more migration north . . .
May 17, 1954 . . . Montgomery bus boycott . . . free-
dom rides . . . sit-ins . . . prominence of CORE . . .
Little Rock . . . more sit-ins, wade-ins, pray-ins . . .
James Meredith . . . March on Washington . . . et cet-
era.

Through all of this one cannot help but discern what,
in the business world, is tantamount to periods of "Bust
and Boom . . . Boom and Bust." Why, after all of these
years, is the Negro not free? Why has the Negro's strug-

gle not taken a more effective, a more *final*, a more existential mode? It is because the Negro has accepted the white man's definition or conceptualization of how to achieve his freedom. By this I do not mean that any single white man or group of white men is directing the Negro's struggle. I mean that Negroes themselves have accepted in theory and practice forms of struggling, or "protesting," that are defined by the *modus operandi* ("the way we do things over here") of the Establishment. In a word, the freedom movement has become *institutionalized*. It is organically involved with and handicapped by the mode of *de facto* politics, economics, and everything else that governs and handicaps this nation. The white Establishment is not going to conceptualize, let alone approve of, a mode of struggle that will lead to the effective and speedy overthrow of the white man's dominant position in society. Anyway, the sheer machinery of the Establishment—the law, politics, economics, government—operates in such a way as to impede, if not prevent outright, any major and speedy success in terms of the Negro's struggle to become free. Witness the amount of time it took to get the Civil Rights Bill through Congress. It will probably be another generation before the provisions in that legislation can be organically enforced. By that time Negroes will not need a Civil Rights Bill.

The *institutionalization* of the Negro struggle is achieved in the following ways.

(a) The Negro struggle is made into a *formal* movement. That is, every effort exerted by Negroes must be approved of, one way or another, by the "legitimate leadership." This puts the Negro in a position where he must reveal what he plans to do before he does it. There are set channels and procedures in and through which the Negro must go whenever and wherever he decides to do something about his oppression. A tendency for the struggle to become *ritualized* ensues. No matter what the situation is, the Negro becomes accustomed to struggling against it in a fashion that is repetitive, and most of all, easily predictable by whites. This makes the struggle *orderly*, which is a prescription set down by whites. In the end a great deal of the effort exerted by Negroes amounts to no more than empty ceremony, a solemn parade, or a turbulent demonstration where Negroes suffer brutality from white mobs, water hoses, and police dogs. Classic examples are the March on Washington, in the first instance, and the Birmingham demonstrations, in the second.

(b) The Negro always has to "sit down and talk." This leads to compromise on whatever he is talking about, which means the Negro's struggle is being arrested. The common form in which this process occurs is the "committee." The committee is appointed by someone (from the white Establishment) who is revered for his nonpartisanship. The committee is composed of people of "good will" and of "high standing" in the society or, better yet, from the community in question. Of late the usual thing is to set up a biracial committee. During the "negotiation," the whites "give in" less than the Negroes. Then, too, the whites have a way of not keeping their promises, meager as they might be. When (as infrequently happens) promises are kept, it takes so l–o–n–g to institute them. Another fact about "negotiation" is that a few of the blacks are usually encouraged to do something that smells like "selling out." This is a clear indication that the Negro's struggle is governed by the traditional mode of American politics—currently quite a few Negro leaders have assumed the role of *race diplomats*. Too many Negroes in positions of leadership play the traditional role of Uncle Tom, only now they are "educated" Uncle Toms and are not so easily detected. They deal with the white-and-black committees in such a way as to protect their own self-interest. Especially in the South, it is not unusual to find Negroes in "high places" who soft-pedal demands for freedom and equality in order to make their own positions secure. In most instances nobody knows it but the "diplomat" and the few whites in question. Traditionally, when the white people of "good will" in the South want to stop Negroes from doing something, or to start something, the pattern has been to call in the local

race diplomats, a Negro doctor, preacher, or college president, and "negotiate." All of this is done *behind the
scenes*. Except in rare cases where the situation becomes
public knowledge (blows wide open), the masses do not
know what is going on until the Negro returns and tells
them that such-and-such a line of action, usually ineffec-
tive, is best for them and is what they are going to do.

The nature of diplomacy, from its historical begin-
nings to the present, proves one thing. A diplomat never
actually represents the entirety of his constituency. The
best he usually does is to represent himself along with
his immediate coterie or peers—his *class* interest. This
allows for an explanation as to why, after the suffering and struggling on the part of all Negroes, only a
few, usually middle class, really benefit.

(c) Every time the Negro does something to achieve
his freedom, the response is, "Let's study the situation."
This means all activity by Negroes must cease while the
"study" is in process. Nine times out of ten, white people conduct the study, or administer it, which is the same
thing. It takes a great deal of money, which, of course,
must come from the white Establishment. What the study
boils down to is this. Whites are going to tell how whatever the Negroes want will create more problems than it
will solve and, above all, about how whites and Negroes
simply cannot get along together. Some white sociolo-
gist, or "authority" on race, and his staff will earn a great

deal of money. The authority gets his "findings" published in one of the journals or magazines with mass circulation. Then he publishes his study in book form, receiving high acclaim, and ultimately, as a consequence of his monumental work, he assumes the chair in social sciences at one of the larger universities or runs for political office. This also applies to the few Negroes who from time to time get the chance to "head" a study. Meanwhile, years have passed. The stockpile of our knowledge on race relations accumulates like debris in the archives of the dead.

(d) "Bring the struggle out of the streets and put it in the courts." First, one must sit and be intimidated by the bigotry of southern courts, local judges and other officials. Then, if one is lucky, one comes up through the state courts and finally to the Supreme Court. This takes years and more money than any single Negro or local group of Negroes can ordinarily afford. An avalanche of litigation and red tape is unavoidable. And still, even if the Supreme Court decides in your favor, there is no certainty on the local level that you are actually going to get what is now legally yours. The adjudication of the Negro's rights works in such a way as to prolong the granting of those rights.

(e) The Negro's struggle to achieve his freedom tends to be conceptualized in mythological terms. Negroes do this as well as whites. The struggle is defined in terms of such mystical measures as: "love those who hate you, the need for understanding . . . suffering . . . forgiveness." We are told that the problem is in the "hearts" of Americans. Those who make speeches employ such phrases as: "Go down Moses" . . . "Go Tell It on the Mountain" . . . "I Have a Dream . . ." Negroes are told that "prayer" is a powerful weapon against oppression, and that "God" is on their side. All of this makes for some fine oratory and, more times than not, sloppy poetry. What it means, in too many instances, is that the Negro has adopted a view toward alleviating his oppression that tends to prolong that oppression. A Christian approach toward solving the race problem can do just so much. Non-violent methods of struggling can do just so much. Then the "law of diminishing returns" sets in. Anyway, Negroes are not living in a land of ancient kings. Singing about "Go Down Moses" and "If I Had a Hammer" might call up in the Negro a powerful sense of his suffering. But it also tends to transport the Negro's concentration *away* from *this* world and *this* time, a world and time that, if he is to become free, he must deal with in an objective, secular fashion. This equally applies to Black Nationalism, Back-to-Africanism, and Black Muslimism. Any "solution" to Negro oppression that does not provide *realistic means* toward that solution is a myth-solution.

The poetic and symbolic rhetoric of the freedom movement often indicates its non-militancy. Therefore the threat of violence in coercing compliance with Negro demands is not being utilized. This is what happened when, because of the very secular language in which John Lewis chose to state Negro demands, his speech was heavily censored at the March on Washington. In addition to this, the progress that Negroes make tends to be *generalized* in such a way that when ONE Negro achieves something, it is played up as if ALL Negroes had achieved it. Sidney Poitier has definitely achieved something. The same goes in the case of Jackie Robinson, Ralph Bunche, and so on. But the rank and file of Negroes have not achieved anything. This type of thinking represents "tokenism" in Negro progress. It is a form of vicarious progress and not real progress.

(f) No matter what the Negro says he wants—civil rights, fair employment, better education, human rights, and so on—the white man, especially the southerner, never fails to bring up the question: "Would you want your daughter or your sister to marry one?" This question seems sufficiently to caution, if not inflame, all whites against integrating Negroes into the mainstream of American democracy.

(g) There is a trend on the part of some civil rights groups to place an undue amount of emphasis on *policy*. More and more the Freedom Movement is becoming involved with bureaucracy. Bureaucracy often confuses communication and impedes progress. The leaders and other personnel of the movement are beginning to look and act like Organization Men. What organizationism does is to coerce every small or local group to conform to policy. This prevents, or limits, spontaneous action and independent thinking. The Negro Freedom Movement tends not to tolerate protest actions or demonstrations that veer from its current policy of non-violence and of not offending or embarrassing white "friends" of the movement. This is known as "Negro Liberalism." Of course, the policy of non-violence and Negro Liberalism is a direct reflection of the influence that the white Establishment has upon the Negro struggle. Negroes go along with this policy because, I am afraid, it is the only one that liberal whites approve of and mainly because Negroes have the same *values* as the white Establishment.

I have already mentioned how John Lewis' March on Washington speech was censored and disapproved of because the speech made a radical departure from the agreed upon policy. Agreed upon by Whom, by What? —by white liberals and Negro liberals who did not want to say or do anything that would "offend" the white Establishment and, most of all, President John F. Kennedy. Another example occurred when one branch of the New York CORE decided to stage a massive automobile "stall-in" on major transportation arteries on the opening day of the World's Fair. There was much debate within as well as between the major civil rights groups. The local chapter of CORE made an effort to go ahead, but the "stall-in" as such was a telling failure. I do not know if any "heads rolled." I do know that the local was suspended from the larger body.

(h) Instead of intensifying the aggression against the wider society, many Negroes feel that they must get themselves ready, that they must "prepare" for integration and equality. They must acquire "good manners" and, in general, they must learn how to "act" before they can expect whites to treat them as human beings. What this means is that too often Negroes assume toward themselves the same attitudes that whites have. Frequently the psychology of the Negro is that of a freak striving to achieve equality with normal people. The "normal people," whites, define the terms of the "freak's" equality. The Negro accepts these terms. He abandons his own qualities, his manners and habits, and strives to imitate the values, habits and behavior patterns of white folks. It is this viewpoint that tends to cover up or usurp every phase of the Negro's struggle for human recognition in America.

Considering everything I have asserted so far, is the current wave of American Negro protest a *revolutionary* movement? The answer is inescapable. There is not now nor has there ever been a black revolution in America.

A revolution, any revolution, is a ruthless program of aggression, on the part of the oppressed masses, against the very foundation of the powers that oppress. A movement with revolutionary intent seeks not to reform certain limited aspects within a society but to destroy or overturn the entire organizational structure. It leaves in its wake the ruins not merely of the one institution that is directly identified with oppression, but also makes havoc of the entire socioeconomic-political complex. True revolutionaries know that it is the *complex* which is ultimately responsible for oppression or freedom. You cannot escape hatred and oppression in a world of hatred and oppression. A world of hatred and oppression has to be reorganized from top to bottom, both materially and psychologically, to rid it of hatred and oppression.

There is no revolutionary *mentality* in America. America, white and black, because of its historical development, does not have the kind of imagination that creates revolution. The leaders, the organizations and groups that are in the forefront of the Negro struggle and which are accepted as legitimate by the white Establishment, are not clamoring so much for individual *liberty* or true freedom as they are for *uniformity* in social status and public treatment (equality). These Negroes want to be accepted in and by white society, not as individual personalities, but as if they were white themselves. They

84

have the same values as white. This attitude necessarily puts a strait jacket on how far the Negro will go in throwing off his oppression. Freedom for the great number of Americans—white and Negro (especially middle-class Negroes)—has a Madison Avenue meaning. It means material comfort. James Meredith, for instance, has repeatedly stated that the main motivation behind his endurance at the University of Mississippi was the very American desire to "get ahead," to be able to function as a lawyer in his Mississippi home town, and to acquire the material comforts propagandized as "common" to our American way of life, just as a white man would do.

I believe that the majority of Negroes want to throw off oppression *within* the context of the American Establishment. The Negro is not yet willing to run the risk of a total assault on the culture, to find that many of the things for which he has fought, and is fighting, will no longer be available, within the socioeconomic and political framework that now characterizes this nation. It is a question of values, namely, *whether it is best to do away completely with oppression as undesirable and find that other desirable values are also done away with, or to "protest" deliberately or unwittingly in such ways as to prolong in one form or another the existence of the race problem, and thereby retain many of the more desirable features of the American system.* This is the real American Dilemma. Contrary to what Gunnar Myrdal asserted in his book, *An American Dilemma,* the vast majority of whites in the United States have never had any guilt feelings about the discrepancy between the American creed and what they actually did in real life. It was only when someone tried to change the status quo significantly that whites became alarmed. It is largely the same today.

There is, on the other hand, a revolutionary force in America. But it is a force locked within itself because it has been, and is, alienated from its own powers—the powers of violence. I am referring to the *black masses,* the ignorant, impoverished, unrefined, bottom-rung Negroes in the South and in the black ghettos of the North. These are the final people. They constitute maybe 90 per cent of the Negroes in this country. These are the people that the white liberals and the Negro middle class will have to deal with. These are the existential Negroes!

Because the Negro's struggle tends to be institutionalized on every level and in all respects, the masses of colored people are largely excluded from receiving any of the gains that the middle-class oriented Negroes are now making. This is true in all but a few isolated instances. One notable exception was the Montgomery Bus Protest Movement. When the deal went down, all—not one or two or a few—ALL Negroes were free to ride the buses in Montgomery. On the other hand, in Birmingham, the masses of Negroes endured the water, the dogs, the brutality of the mobs. When the deal went down they had nothing concrete to show for it but their scars. I believe a few (probably two) Negroes got jobs and a few lunch counters (probably five) were desegregated.

The Birmingham situation is not the exception but the rule. Until the violence, or the potential violence, of the masses of Negroes is felt throughout the nation, there will be no Negro revolution. We will be experiencing a revolution when civil, economic, and human oppression, in a very concrete way, is lifted from the lives of the black masses. But this will involve much more than just a "black" revolution. It will be an *American* Revolution.

Whether one describes the current activities of Negroes in this country as the "Civil Rights Movement," the "Freedom Movement," the "Negro Upheaval," or by any other phrase is not purely a question of semantics. There *is* something going on. There is a great deal of activity, a tremendous amount of noise. Since there are people—black and white—who refer to all of this as "The Negro (or Black) Revolution," it is not enough to show that they are in error. One has the responsibility of trying to understand what the term means to the people who employ it in relationship to what is actually happening. Most of all, one must unearth the reason *why* people use this term when its real meaning does not apply to the situation.

I believe it was around 1960 when Louis E. Lomax, Negro reporter and author, published an article called "The Negro Revolt" in one of the better "slick" magazines. The article was then made into a book under the same title. Largely the "revolt" that Mr. Lomax was talking about had to do with the younger generation of Negroes revolting against the older type of Negro leadership. The young, predominantly college-enrolled, Negroes ("sit-inners") were knocking down the orthodox leaders as being too slow and conservative, and they were beginning to take things into their own hands. A new militancy developed.

The term "Negro Revolution" seemed to have come into prominence subsequent to Lomax's book. As time passed and more and more Negroes took to the streets, the term began to be used by the press with mounting frequency. I believe also that the Cuban Revolution had a suggestive impact upon all of us, especially white Americans, so that the term slipped into the press to describe what Negroes were doing, although at the time we were quite unaware of the psychology involved and although there was to be sure a world of difference between what Castro did and what Negroes were undertaking. To realize this is to see clearly what the press, either consciously or unconsciously, was and is doing in labeling the activities of contemporary Negroes as the "Negro Revolution."

The whole thing begins to make sense. A pattern begins to emerge. American white people tend to view *anything* the Negro does to achieve his freedom as being "revolutionary." It is at once a fear reaction, a sort of racial reflex response in lieu of protecting their dominant position, and a conscious or unconscious attempt to deceive the Negro so that he will not really *become* revolutionary. If Negroes can be made to *think* that they are being revolutionary, they will become satisfied with what they are getting or will become confused as to the exact nature of what it takes to really make them free, and what it is really like to *be* free. In a very real sense for a great majority of American whites, an example of the "Negro Revolution" is when one or two Negroes, as a consequence of mass demonstrations, sit-ins, lie-ins, and so on, receive employment as construction workers. Negroes, rhapsodized by the mass media and perhaps by the intoxicating effect of assuming a collective consciousness, are lulled or excited into viewing their behavior also as the "Black Revolution."

Another factor which lies behind the rhetoric of the "Negro Revolution" is *sensationalism*. Five years ago, judging from the mass media, one would have difficulty saying for certain that Negroes, except for rapists, murderers, thieves and other criminals, lived in America. To-

day the "news" about Negroes gets fantastic presentation via radio, television, newspapers, and magazines.

At last the Negro is valuable commercial property. The
"Black Gold Rush" is on! So much is being published
about the Negro that one simply cannot keep up with it
all. *Life, Time, Newsweek, Look, Saturday Review,
Harper's,* and on down the line. The publishing houses
are rolling the stuff out. I will hazard that during the last
five years more "Negro material" has been published by
the American press than in any previous twenty-year
period. Most of it is little more than garbage. But who
cares? It sells. Noticeably, the *New York Times* began
to carry much more news about Negroes shortly after its
West Coast edition folded.

At no time in the history of publishing, not even during the left-wing thirties, have so many Negro writers
been able to get their works into print as during the past
five years. Whites also are exploiting the unprecedented
commercialism of Negro subject matter. In fact, there is
an "underground" animosity developing between Negro
and white writers. Despite the Negro's superior knowledge of the subject, whites seem to be "cashing in" on
Negro material with much less difficulty from publishers,
reviewers, and the public than most Negroes. Hollywood
has made *Black Like Me,* written by a white man, into a
movie. Nobody, to my knowledge, has dared to film Ralph
Ellison's *Invisible Man.*

With reference to the so-called "Black Revolution" it-self, whites are infiltrating the movement. Wherever there is a Negro sit-in, wade-in, pray-in, or any sort of protest or demonstration, whites are to be found among the ranks. I would guess that at least one-fourth of the marchers on Washington were whites. Even the Black Muslims, whose attitude toward whites is unmistakable, are plagued by Caucasians clamoring to "join" them!

I know there are some white people who are genuinely dedicated to the cause of freedom. I also know that there are too many whites who are aligning themselves with Negroes simply because they have a pathological craving for attention and publicity. Many whites are downright jealous of the attention Negroes are currently receiving via the mass media. They join the movement because, I am afraid, they have no other means of acquiring recog-nition. I am reminded of a young white man who is, or was, an official of one of the civil rights organizations. The young man was brought into court, tried, and given a short sentence for civil disobedience. He sat down on the floor of the court room and refused to be moved. The judge advised him to leave or be charged with contempt. The white zealot refused to budge and called the entire court, including the judge, members of the Ku Klux Klan. Growing impatient and peeved, the judge added ninety more days to the sentence, whereupon the zealot went into a tantrum and had to be dragged from the floor of the court. He received plenty of attention. The next day his actions were reported by the papers and the radio and television networks.

Since it is now receiving more publicity than at any other time in history, the Negro movement, in too many instances, becomes a bandwagon for white crackpots and misfits. This is equally true of some Negroes who are *playing* revolution. They are jumping on the bandwagon. There occurred an incident in Harlem where some Negroes were picketing a small restaurant owned by a Puerto Rican. Working there were one Negro dishwasher in the rear and three light-skinned Puerto Ricans up front. The Negroes were demonstrating to have a dark-skinned Negro employed up front. Unbeknown to the public there was some fuss as to who was the leader of this demonstration. There were two preachers contending for "leadership" and they were at each other's throats. Suddenly a policeman informed one of them that he had to move his automobile. At that moment the newsmen and television cameras converged upon the second "leader." I watched him on television. Obviously, he *knew* his picture would be in the papers, and he *knew* his "statement" would appear in the press. He was so *aware* and *proud* that his face was being televised. That man should not have been the leader of that demonstration any more than Ross Barnett should have been the Governor of Mississippi. *Dead water and dead sand contending for the up-per hand.*

As long as the masses of black people remain dispossessed, as long as the American Establishment does not provide an avenue through which the ignorant, utterly deprived portion of Negroes, and whites, can realize a sense of personal dignity and social worth in terms of the humanity of man, this nonsense can go on. It may never end.

The sensationalism and commercialism of the Freedom Movement serve to obscure what is really happening. There is some progress being made, but how much and where it is all leading is difficult to ascertain at the present time. No one knows what all of this is unleashing in the emotional chambers of white southerners. Mississippi, for instance, is a virtual Nazi state awaiting the "Final Solution." Is anyone preparing for the worst between blacks and whites in the South, and North, except cops and racists? We are too busy being sensational and making money.

Without bringing in the international situation, which limits whatever analysis one might make, there seems to be a new deprivation, an excitement vacuum in America which the current Negro upheaval is consummating. Secretly we are on pins and needles waiting for the next headline, the next radio announcement, the next bloody photograph in the tabloids, waiting for the televised bar-

barity between blacks and whites to boom into the bore-
dom of our living rooms. Obscenity. This is what we
are reduced to. It is not horror that we feel when we see
in the media black men and women being maimed in the
streets. It is prurience. The pornography of black men
and women bodily clashing with white men and women.
To wit, a large proportion of Americans, especially whites,
perceive the intermingling of Negroes and Caucasians as
something extremely lewd. To witness it acted out via
the mass media, not in love but in hate and violence,
constitutes a vicarious ecstasy of the most depraved nature. Not too long ago the *New York Times* printed on
the front page a photograph of white men in St. Augus-
tine, Florida, beating a group of Negroes with bottles
and sticks. What has come over us! I am a Negro and I
will not submit my body to that kind of twisted pain.
How can people participate in that form of race-sex orgy?

At a New York rally held shortly after the Cleveland,
Ohio, demonstration where a white minister was accidentally killed by throwing himself in the path of a bull-
dozer, Malcolm X refused to declare a period of silent
prayer in reverence for the minister's death. A white man
from the audience had suggested the period of silence.
Malcolm X refused to honor the request. He stated that
unnumbered Negroes have been and are being murdered
and nobody has offered up a prayer for them. While this

is not altogether true, Malcolm's attitude had a tremendous effect upon the audience, most of which were bottom-rung, lower-class Negroes. They leaped to their feet and cheered.

I discovered something during that rally. Malcolm was apocalyptic. His words were brute, concrete, secular, and he *communicated* with the masses. Whether you or I like it or not, he could have become the most *followed* Negro of our times. He was an anti-charisma that recriminated radical whites and middle-class Negroes, and he electrified the common masses. Here are his words:

> In America . . . whites go around with the attitude "I am white" in the sound of their voices, in the essence of their beings. . . . It is impossible for a white person to believe in capitalism and not believe in racism. . . . You can't talk this "Negro Revolution" jive to me when you're not ready for it. When the deal is down, most of you aren't.

Malcolm X was probably the only Negro who (whether he was or not) talked like a *real* revolutionary.

At the time that Malcolm made the foregoing statement, Drew Pearson was calling Dick Gregory and Adam C. Powell too "radical." He said that whites were forming a "solid block" against Negroes, and that Negroes were losing "understanding and sympathy" from whites in the North as well as in the South.

Precisely! It can be this kind of attitude, among other things, that might bring an abortive close to the current stage in the Freedom Movement. Unless one is insane, he hopes it does not come to that. Nevertheless it seems as if Drew Pearson's attitude (or was it an observation?) is the growing tendency among more and more whites. And I fear we will not become sufficiently aware of the meaning of what is happening in and to us until it is too late. The current struggle constitutes the *precipitating* stage. Unless we do something now, one way or another, to free those millions of blacks whom I have spoken of as "Existential Negroes," there may not be a revolution, but there will definitely be Armageddon.

Another Man Done Gone: the Death of Malcolm X

A great man is precisely a beginner because he sees further than others, and desires things more strongly than others. . . . He is a hero. But he is not a hero in the sense that he can stop, or change, the natural course of things, but in the sense that his activities are the conscious and free expression of this inevitable and unconscious course. Herein lies all his significance; herein lies his whole power. But this significance is colossal, and the power is terrible.

GEORGE PLEKHANOV
The Role of the Individual in History

Three days before the assassin's bullets ripped his body full of holes and blood sprayed the floor of the Audubon Ballroom, I walked the streets of Harlem, up and down the infamous Avenues, Seventh, Eighth, Lenox, stopping here and there for a drink, Silver Rail, Sugar Ray's, Braddock, Hoo Tai's, The Big Apple—two-for-one, three-for-one, four-for-one, lingering, listening, observing, pick-

ing up bits of conversation, arguments, damnation to white men . . . in all of this one heard the name of Malcolm X many, many times . . . "he's slick," "he's politically ambitious," "he's damn right," "he lays it on the line," "he wouldn't talk like that down South," "he's a shady character," "he's my main man." . . . Among the varying opinions about him, and though no one seemed to know exactly why, one thing was constant—"Malcolm X is a genius," "Malcolm X is Great!"

It is altogether puzzling to hear people refer to a man as "great" when the man's influence barely reaches beyond his immediate habitat.

The puzzle begins to unravel when one considers the fact that the man had arrived at a condition in his life where he was no longer an agent of any established or even slightly structured institution, group, movement, or sphere of influence. In a part of the world where man's behavior, ideas and thoughts are more and more becoming so affected by organizations, by policy, by mass pressure, bureaucratic protocol, and by "acceptable" rules and regulations that it is virtually impossible to do anything without the aid of, or at least, without the sanction of some kind of institution—in this type of world, where there are no more frontiers, Malcolm X broke away from everything and stood alone, or at least, stood *independently*. He opened up, expanded, transcended himself, and with reference to the Negro struggle, became a frontiersman.

Specifically, after he broke from the Black Muslims, he offered his aid to many groups and persons, but he refused to *join* any one or to accept an official *job* or perform a certain *designated* function for any one. This made him *free*. Unlike Dr. King, Wilkins, Farmer, and the rest, Malcolm rose above being "replaced," for he occupied no office, no position, no specified capacity. This made it impossible for anybody or anything—including the Establishment itself—to program or even influence the programming of his activities, for in truth, he was *outside* of the Establishment. He was a man AT LARGE.

Although his original status had been acquired in and through the institutional machinery of the Black Muslims and his role had been defined by that organization, Malcolm transcended the status structure of the Black Muslims and acquired, in spite of rather than because of that organization, a status that was greater than anything the Black Muslims could bestow upon him. After he quit the Muslims, he owed no one for his status. This enabled him to choose, at will, the nature of the role he would play in the Negro struggle. Considering Malcolm's background, it is not unusual for such a man to become a frontiersman or an outlaw, but for such a person to *succeed* at it is to possess that rare, enigmatic quality men call "greatness."

It is a relatively easy task to describe how a man attains greatness, *after* he has attained it. We can, given the historical context, theorize certain prescriptions for greatness, but we cannot *predict* who is capable of executing such prescriptions and, in fact, becoming great! There is little fruit in going back and outlining how Malcolm X got to be great. Since greatness does not automatically make one a revolutionary, what was it about Malcolm X that made him dangerous?

His actual followers consisted of but a handful of people in Harlem. But his sympathizers were the entire Harlem community. I have stated that Malcolm owed his status to no one. This is not altogether true. He owed his status to his sympathizers who were potential followers. The sympathizers of Malcolm X consisted of Negroes who lived a barbarous existence—lower-class, inarticulate, predominantly ignorant or semi-ignorant men and women and teenagers who make up approximately 90 per cent not merely of the Harlem population but of the Negro population in the United States. In other words, Malcolm's power stemmed from Negroes like himself. Only the people, the beat and hopeless masses, could have rendered him powerless and sent him back into anonymity.

This made the potential nature of his power *unlimited,* for only the masses are the potential possessors of absolute power. Their power stems from the congregated might of their violence!

Malcolm was not merely a onetime leader or hero. Rather he was an *identification image* of the masses. He was not somebody who was merely "interested in" or "dedicated to" their uplift; he was one of them himself. As with himself, he showed the masses that their ignorance, hopelessness, their depraved and preyed-upon existence was due to the conditions and forces that other men, predominantly white, had created and maintained within the realm of social reality; that their troubled milieux were inextricably linked with the institutionalization of power in this country; that in order to do away with their private agonies, they had to fashion such agonies into public issues in a way that would destroy or reorganize the entire power structure of America.

To be independent of virtually all institutional checks and controls and at the same time to be the identification image of the majority of Harlem Negroes (as well as of the majority of the American Negroes) makes one the potential heir to the possibilities of unlimited power. To be these things and to talk like Malcolm X is to be revolutionary, and dangerous! Dangerous to everybody—except the masses, of course; dangerous to the NAACP, CORE, Martin Luther King and Company, the Black Muslims, and to the Establishment itself.

Had Malcolm gone into politics, he might be alive

today. At least this would have reduced his power potential along with his militant revolutionism, for then he would have become subject to the structures and definitions of whatever political office or institutional role he would have to function in.

Let's face it, the aims and the programs of all the civil rights groups are not dangerous to the entire American system but merely to certain "undemocratic" segments of it. The program of the Black Muslims is dangerous only to Black Muslims—for they have a dead-end program. That's why they are the least feared and least bothered group in America. Only one man stood as the potential and inevitable foe to every institution that goes to make up the complex structure of our society.

Never before in the history of this country (or perhaps once, only) have the semiliterate, down-beat blacks of the poolrooms, street corners, dance halls, liquor joints, and filthy ghettos found a man in whom they could place so much of their confidence. He was indeed one of them in every way. He was the only man, black or white, who could articulate, in the living language of the ghetto, the intimate agonies of the people, and transform them into a weapon of revolution. And he was slowly but surely on the road to doing just that. Malcolm X was an existential Negro who came to possess the rare gift of metamorphosing others like himself from depraved and hopeless men locked *in* themselves to enlightened men freed *for* themselves.

Who engineered his death, whether it was actually the Muslims or some aspect of the Establishment, or even some outside international plotters, is not the question. What we must ascertain is who "benefited" by his removal. The answer is clear. Everybody benefited except the masses. The various civil rights groups and business interests that are striving for the integration of the Negro into the mainstream of this society no longer have a "lone wolf" riding their backs to castigate them for collaborating against the human interest of the riffraff masses.

The reactionary whites of the South and the North are no longer threatened with a Negro whose potential was that of rousing the black masses to self-defense by violence. The Muslims are relieved that a force, which tended to enlighten rather than to dumbfound and exploit the black masses has been removed. It is the *function* of Malcolm's death that is depressing and pitiful.

There is no one around who can fill his shoes. Because, as a type of Negro, he was an anomaly. In order to articulate the agonies of the masses into public issues that are meaningful for *them*, one cannot be merely "from" or "for" the masses, one must be *of* the masses. The Negro masses are a very distrustful lot and, at the same time, are burning with undirected hostility which they'd as soon let loose upon themselves as upon a so-called leader who might accidentally slip in the mere way he speaks to them. In order to be effective, one who is of the masses must possess not only the sense of reality *peculiar* to the masses but also that rare ability to *convince* the outer society of this reality.

Malcolm's sister has expressed her intentions of assuming her brother's place. As time goes on no doubt others will enter the competition. But the most his sister or anyone can do is occupy his physical office and deflect some Negroes from the Black Muslims into the clamoring legions of the integrationists, or start some kind of cult.

In reality, phenomenologically, the removal of Malcolm X was the obliteration of his "place." His status was peculiar to him and him alone. He was that rare kind of personage of the masses which societies produce once every fifty to a hundred years. For his kinsmen the loss is total. All that is left to us now is to bury him, and perhaps utter . . . *another man done gone.*

CHAPTER 4

BLOOD OF THE LAMB

THE ORDEAL OF JAMES BALDWIN

> *Singing Hallelujah!*
> *Blood of the lamb!*
> *Let your voices rise!* . . .
> FROM A SONG BESSIE SMITH
> USED TO SING.

*This paper was written during the early part of 1964.
James Baldwin was then at the zenith (and decline) of
his fame in America. His name was on the lips of almost
everybody who read serious literature in this country
(probably less than ½ of 1 per cent of our population).
Great numbers of whites were raving about Baldwin as
not only the literary genius of the times (a period of*

about three years) but also as the most astute interpreter and spokesman of the plight of twenty million black Americans. While many Negroes followed suit, there were a great many more who spoke and wrote about Baldwin with sheer hatred and jealousy. For instance, Sylvester Leaks, a Harlem writer, whose writing does not equal his political rabble-rousing, published a "letter" (Freedomways, *Winter* 1963) *called "James Baldwin—I Know His Name." This was nothing more than an impoverished attempt to discredit Baldwin's genius, on the one hand, and a downright expression of sourgrape jealousy on the other. All of this—this essay as well as many similar comments by others—made me mad. All of it! So I decided to write* Blood of the Lamb. . . .

I

The romance of our times is the one currently going on between white Americans and a highly photogenic Negro. The Negro is James Baldwin. I am not being giddy. When I say *romance,* I mean just that, I mean *love affair.*

No other Negro writer has ever been admired by whites as Baldwin is. Nor has any Negro ever before been so popular in the American press. Within the last year, Baldwin's name and face have appeared in almost every worth-while (and some not so worth-while) publication in America—from the crisp, pseudofactual pages of *Time* magazine to the slick, feminine sheets of *Harper's Bazaar*. Although Negro leaders, academicians, intellectuals, and writers are familiar with Baldwin's works, more white people than Negroes *love* him, especially liberals and white women. Many Negroes, especially writers, express ambivalence over Baldwin. Quite a few of them envy or "put him down" for no reason I can see other than that he is famous and successful. On the other hand, I have yet to meet a white person who has not expressed his "empathy" for Baldwin; who has not confessed his rapture over *Another Country* or his longing for the eloquent, baptismal flames of *The Fire Next Time*. With white Americans no other Negro writer, past or contemporary, stands a chance, be he Ralph Ellison, Langston Hughes, John Killens, or the late Richard Wright.

What lies behind this?

Much too much has been written about Baldwin. But for all that it is worth, hardly anybody has probed the nature of Baldwin's phenomenal appeal to white Americans, and the ideological atmosphere that has made possible his affluent popularity in the American press. Norman Mailer has scratched the surface somewhat. Irving Howe's discussion (September 14, 1963), "From Richard Wright to James Baldwin," over WBAI showed insight, but did not go far beyond the usual "literary criticism."* Julian Mayfield's "And Then Came Baldwin" (*Freedomways*, Spring 1963), and Colin MacInnes' "Dark Angel" (*Encounter*, July 1964), are the best essays I have seen so far. Indeed, Baldwin has enchanted and outraged the American *literati* with his great, eloquent syntax, his seemingly boundless honesty, and with his terrible but well-disciplined anger. At least one white writer I know of has imitated Baldwin's honesty with a fair degree of success. Norman Podhoretz's article, "My Negro Problem—And Ours," (*Commentary*, February 1963), reflects the current "climate of honesty and soul searching" on the race problem by blacks and whites that I am certain Baldwin's writings have precipitated. Beyond this, however, in the avalanche of articles and reviews on Baldwin, there has been too much talk about "style," too much commercialism and mechanical description, too much false imitation, too much petty jealousy, and not enough *analysis*. In his envoi to *A Quarter Century of UnAmericana*, edited by Charlotte Pomerantz, Baldwin wrote:

> *I* . . . does not refer so much to the man called Baldwin as it does to the reality which has produced me, a reality with which I live, and from which most Americans spend all their time in flight.

* This discussion was later published as an essay titled "Black Boys and Native Sons" in *Dissent* (Autumn 1963), for which Mr. Howe serves as editor.

II

There is a phantom, an enigma that haunts most of
Baldwin's writing. The "enigma" is Baldwin's father.
When I read *Go Tell It on the Mountain*, I found it
difficult at times to discern whether the narrator was
talking about the principal or about his father. The two
figures, in certain passages, seemed to merge, blur, and
break away in a most laborious rhythm, like tortured
lovers. In *Giovanni's Room* the hero saunters through his
love affair, but not without haunting recollections of the
father. The father seems to have something to do with
the hero's predicament; yet one cannot completely figure
out what it is. Again, in many of Baldwin's essays
(*Notes of a Native Son* in particular), the father is discussed and rediscussed, always in a vague, rather metaphysical fashion. No matter how smoothly the writing
flows, there is an *uneasiness* that bores through whenever
the father is brought up.

The constant involvement with the father constitutes
a "hang-up." Baldwin wanted so desperately to love and
be loved by his father; but, alas, he was shipwrecked
upon a sea of fear, pity, and hate. In one passage, in
Notes of a Native Son, Baldwin writes that his father
was ". . . very handsome . . . proud . . . chilling in the
pulpit and indescribably cruel in his personal life. . . .

Yet there was something which lent him his tremendous power . . . blackness and beauty." In the same essay Baldwin states clearly that he hated his father, and that his father was certainly "the most bitter man" he had ever met.

To what extent, in Baldwin's mind and in reality, is the father, as much as the Harlem ghetto, responsible for Baldwin's feeling of inadequacy? My opinion is that the father symbolizes the phallic deprivation of Baldwin's childhood and the, to use his word, *conundrum* of his manhood. And Baldwin has had to labor with this "hang-up." Being a writer, he has sought clarification and resolution in the best way he knew how: by writing about it.

But the father enigma goes further than Baldwin's biological father. In the struggling days of Baldwin's career, it extended or projected itself onto the most powerful black man in literature, Richard Wright. Why not? After all, we get glimpses of Baldwin's father as being a "pork chop," Bible-belt cripple of the white man's world, a mendicant of the Protestant ethics of white supremacy. "I could see him," writes Baldwin about his father, "locked up in his terrors; hating and fearing every living soul including his children. . . . I began to wonder what it could have felt like for such a man to have had nine children whom he could barely feed. . . . He used to make jokes about our poverty, which never . . . seemed very funny to us. . . ." And as the father lay dying, Baldwin describes him as: "All shriveled and still, like a little black monkey!"

On the other hand, Richard Wright was a black power structure unto himself. There was nothing weak about him. He rejected the communists at a time when it was not altogether fashionable to do so; he thumbed his nose at the Confederate flag; wrote like a pneumatic drill; went to Europe and had people like Sartre, Camus, Gide, and Nkrumah come to his home and listen to what he had to say. What better symbol would a young Negro wish to identify with. Many budding Negro writers thought, and still think, of Wright as their hero, their idol.

It is also interesting to note that Baldwin's early life reminds one in many ways of the early days of Richard Wright. Both Wright and Baldwin were born in poverty; both had a drive to become somebody and met with disapproval from their families as well as from their particular Negro communities. The only thing Baldwin could become in Harlem was a preacher, and he did this to some degree in an effort to win the love of his father and at the same time he did it to compete with his father. The ministry, however, proved to be little more than a minor balm for Baldwin's agony. So, after his father died he left Harlem, and moved to, or better still, "hung out" in Greenwich Village. His escape from the ghetto may be compared to Richard Wright's flight from Mississippi. Both later exiled themselves in Europe with no intention of ever coming back.

Baldwin's "hang-up" with Wright, however, stemmed not from the mere fact that he identified with and idolized Wright. Owing to the flaw in the relationship between himself and his father which was, in Baldwin's words, "a murderous relationship," owing to this flaw, Baldwin wanted something more than identification with Wright; he longed for something deeper; he wanted from Wright what he did not get from his own father. Although the following words are spoken by Baldwin with reference to his father, they very well express what he desired of Richard Wright—"What I really wanted was for him to *love* me. For me to be able to *prove* myself to him."

The crisis of this desire occurred when Baldwin went to Europe. Nothing happened. Or, in Baldwin's mind, what did happen was closer to denial or indifference than to love on Wright's part of the encounter. Baldwin had written a piece called "Everybody's Protest Novel," in which he took Wright (*Native Son*) to task, and Wright considered the piece a direct affront. Rebuffed and angered, Baldwin took up his pen and, with hydrochloric pathos, dealt an avenging blow to perhaps the only black man he ever really loved. "Many Thousand Gone" and "Alas, Poor Richard" resolved (or dissolved), for the time being, the mean affair with Wright in Europe.

The pater-fallacy and the "hang-up" with Richard Wright are not dichotomous; they are interdynamic, they make up a syndrome. This is evident in Baldwin's encounter with the Black Muslim leader, Elijah Muhammad. Several times in that essay, *The Fire Next Time*, Baldwin tells us that Elijah impressed him like the father. "He made me think of my father and me as we might have been if we had been friends." And at one moment during the course of the meeting, Baldwin slipped into an adolescent reverie: "I felt very close to him (Elijah) and really wished to be able to love and honor him as a witness, an ally, and a father." But when Elijah's smile seemed to ask: "Whose little boy are you?" Baldwin could not respond, "Why, I am your little boy," as he had done twenty years before because, Baldwin writes, "There are some things that one cannot do twice."

There is another ingredient in Baldwin's syndrome. It is the fact (and myth) of Baldwin's color. He is heavy-laden with the immense agony of being black. Always, more than anything else, it has been this "hang-up" that has made havoc with Baldwin's soul, first as a man, second as a writer, and third as an autonomous individual.

Baldwin was, or is, a rather short, puny and dark Negro. According to white standards (which are predominantly the standards of the Negro world), he is ugly. He was not only rejected and mocked by the white world but, more significantly, he was hated and derided by other Negroes and most of all by his own father. Thus, Baldwin hated Negroes because they hated him. He hated his father because his father first hated him. Psychologically, he embraced the white world and especially identified with young, handsome, blond males. Realizing, however, that this was no solution to his agony, he confessed that one day he could hate white people as much as he did Negroes, that is, if God did not change his life.

We must understand that, to Baldwin, the race problem has been *his* problem. While it is easy to see, in everything written by a Negro on the subject of race, that which is universal to all Negroes, it is more difficult to discern that which is uniquely the writer's own personal suffering. To repeat what Norman Mailer has already observed, in everything Baldwin writes, more than about anyone or anything else, Baldwin is writing about Baldwin! His ordeal has been to transcend the cripple in himself and the realities which have produced or allowed that cripple to develop in a so-called healthy civilization.

III

When Baldwin went to Europe, he was confused, a "cripple," and, to use his phrase, he was crippled both as "an honest man and a good writer." And he knew it.

During the days in Greenwich Village, he admitted that he got into trouble with everybody, cops, landladies, white girls, pimps, faggots, the lot. Recalling how he felt prior to his flight to Paris, Baldwin says: "I could not be certain whether I was really rich or really poor, really white or really black, really male or female, really talented or a fraud, really strong or merely stubborn. . . ." In Europe, he hoped for some kind of salvation; he hoped for wholeness, or for what some people call "identity."

What happened to Baldwin the eight years in Europe is best described in his essays—*Notes of a Native Son*, and in an article that appeared in the *New York Times Book Review* shortly after he returned to this country. One thing is certain, Baldwin had expected too much of Europe. His meeting with Wright, for instance, had proved disillusioning at the least. Moreover, the general climate of Europe was not so outgoing to Baldwin at first. He was an anxiety-ridden man, disgruntled and hard to get along with. He was poor and he was suffering. And his ego was bleeding from self-hatred for, since he was "black" and "ugly," how could he hate his race without loathing himself? He admits that oftentimes he was drunk and lonely. He plundered dives and streets inhabited by beat men and women, pimps, faggots, prostitutes. In all of this, however, Baldwin had one thing in his favor. Perhaps the most important thing for any writer to remember when he has sunk to a low level, and the one thing that sets a writer apart from the dereliction in which he finds himself, is the constant *sense of himself as a writer*, for this is the only thing that can save him. Baldwin had (and still has) this inside himself.

Somewhere in a lonely room in the middle of Europe, Baldwin labored over his typewriter, while in the background the plaintive, atavistic blues of Bessie Smith stirred and soothed his soul.

> *Woke up this morning*
> *When chickens was crowing 'fore day*
> *Felt on my pillow*
> *My man had gone away . . .*
> *By his pillow he left a note*
> *Reading: "I'm sorry, Jane,*
> *You got my goat . . .*

And he struck a chord somewhere in his psyche. Deep within he wrestled with the ambiguous illusions that plagued him, and which had driven him beyond the physical and psychological regions of his native land. In this alien region, Baldwin met himself face to face.

> *Some people call me a hobo*
> *Some call me a bum*
> *Nobody knows my name*
> *Nobody knows what I've done.*

When I read *Giovanni's Room* I knew Baldwin had achieved what all writers must long for, the mastery of the contradictory powers within himself. It is by these powers that one is consumed or one is consummated. *Giovanni's Room* was not only an unnoticed masterpiece in literary style, eloquence, and finesse, it was also a conquest of the nameless fear that lurks in the hearts of all men and women, the dark, existential riddle of our nature that makes us tremble with ontological terror when we are in the arms of those we dare love.

> *I'm as good as any woman in your town*
> *I ain't no high yellow*
> *I'm a deep bitter brown*
> *I'm going to drink good moonshine*
> *And run these browns down.*

James Baldwin had come of age. Meanwhile, he was also working on *Another Culture, Another Country*, which has been released as *Another Country*. But before he finished that novel, he knew Europe had done all it could do for him. The old "hang-ups" had been more or less transcended, all except one—the most agonizing one —the "hang-up" of being a black American. The Negroes and Africans that Baldwin met in Europe ("Encounter on the Seine") had offered no solace for his problem. Europe offered no solace. In a secluded, all blond village where no black man had ever been ("Stranger in the Village"), Baldwin discovered that the guilt and immorality, the sense of humiliation he had internalized in this country for being a Negro, lived yet within *him*, and would forever leap out to attack him no matter where he was. Flight could not assuage the sickness that was his color. He had to return to the scene of the crime, return to the soil where the fires that had produced him were ablaze. For Baldwin, the problem of his color was indigenous to American soil, and it was therefore in America that it must be fought out ("A Question of Identity").

> *See that long lonesome road*
> *Lord, you know it's got to end.**

So, Baldwin returned, a native son, to wage one of the most heart-rending literary struggles for his dignity to which we have ever paid so much attention. And what has happened?

IV

A romance has ensued. A perverse love affair between white Americans, especially the communications industry, and James Baldwin. It is marvelous, for such a

---

* The above lines and those preceding are from a song Bessie Smith used to sing, "The Young Woman Blues."

public love affair with a black man is unprecedented. Yet it is hazardous, not only for whites but for Baldwin as well. An analysis of the social and psychological ingredients, precisely on the part of the whites, is revealing and alarming.

A full page advertisement in the *New York Times Book Review* (June 17, 1963) contained a large photograph of James Baldwin. In big, black capital letters running beside Baldwin's photograph are these words:

> ACTUALLY I DON'T WANT TO
> MARRY YOUR DAUGHTER.
> I JUST WANT TO GET YOU
> OFF MY BACK.

A significant statement for all Negroes. More significant, however, is why this statement appeals to so many white Americans; so many liberals, both men and women. It is the "promise" of a Negro who has been called "effeminate." It seems that American whites are disposed to love, yea, to suffer with Baldwin not in spite of, but *because* of his lack of "masculine aggressiveness." In the psyches of most white people, Baldwin does not symbolize the historic fear of the great, black phallus which lurks to rape and pillage. This is why whites feared Richard Wright (or fear any aggressive Negro). Dick, in their minds, in their emotions, was perceived as a powerful, black phallus, threatening their guilt-ridden, lily-white world. On the other hand, Baldwin is a sweet, exotic, black boy who cries for mother love (nay, *father* love!) somewhere out in the metaphysical realms of being. Indeed, *Time* magazine (May 17, 1963) described him as "effeminate" in a rather compassionate way. Baldwin "is a nervous . . . almost fragile figure, filled with frets and fears. He is effeminate in manners, drinks . . . smokes cigarettes in chains . . . loses his audience with overblown arguments."

It is immensely revealing that the first Negro to get his face on a full page of the very feminine *Harper's Bazaar* (April 1963) is James Baldwin. The wrinkles of his lips and the pores of his dark skin are intimately revealed. Across from the photograph, on the opposite page, is a three column article: "Letter From a Prisoner." It is supposed to be about or *on* Baldwin. It begins with "Call me Ishmael," and goes on in a senseless jargon about "Black and White," "I and You," "They and We," and some mystical, moral "voice" speaking both for and to "Us and Them." Sheer nonsense! The article is not signed. I know, however, that a white woman wrote it. I also know that *Harper's Bazaar* was very particular about selecting the "right" person to write the kind of slick, effeminate nonsense they wanted. For instance, of all the writers, black and white, who could have said something mean-

ingful—Ellison, Algren, Lillian Smith—they came up
with "Secret Ghostwriter OOX" who not only knows
nothing about Baldwin, the race problem, but who does
not give a damn.

What all of this adds up to is that the American "literary mafia" is bootlegging, or better yet, *prostituting*,
James Baldwin in the wide open. The "compassion and
sympathy" whites feel for the "suffering boy" stems from
the white man's denial of the black man's masculinity,
which whites fear and secretly envy. "We can love Baldwin because he will not screw our daughters," says the
white man. "We can, at last, publicly go to bed with a
Negro, have him soothe our guilt and we his wounds,
without actually giving up anything of our sweat, sinew
and loins." This is probably the most accurate psychoan-
alytic formula for the readiness with which white men
and women open their arms to James Baldwin.

Even white "moderates" (southerners) who find it impossible to accept the Negro as a human being say they
"sympathize" with Baldwin; they feel they can "talk"
with him more than with any other Negro. There is
something weird about the whole affair. Several white
acquaintances have called my attention to the photograph
of Baldwin which accompanied the advertisement for *The
Fire Next Time* and have compared James Baldwin's smile
with Mona Lisa's. And they were drawn to him.

V

Sociologically, the national character of the white man in America is ripe for James Baldwin. With the Negro upheaval that is sweeping the country, whites have no alternative but to accept and put on display a man such as Baldwin who speaks of love, torture, agony and forgiveness. Simply, the national character of America is effeminate! And here, by *effeminate*, I am not so much referring to sex (although one may do well to include it) as I am to political, social, and moral spinelessness. This is especially true in the area of our lives where black is clashing with white. The national, state, and local officials of this country have done (and are still doing) everything possible to withhold from the Negro the full rights and dignities of a citizen, of a human being. Some of us are trying, but our efforts are gainsaid by our psychology. The leadership in Washington lacks backbone for decisive, authoritative action. When Kennedy was alive, he and his administration had to be pushed, had to "politic around" until "mobs and dogs clashed in the streets." John F. Kennedy proposed a Civil Rights Bill, and all hell broke loose. He went on radio and pleaded with us that we were and are facing a "moral crisis." No such thing! We were and are facing a crisis of the power structure in American race relations. Any sycophant knows that the honest, forthright thing which this crisis necessitates is a thorough change in the way POWER is distributed on the basis of color in this country.

But the white man—north and south—is acting, for the most part, in the tradition of the Uncle Tom epoch, when the Negroes themselves did not select their leader but the white men did it for them. Repeatedly, I hear whites (and some middle-class Negroes) telling me that Baldwin is a leader, or that he is verbalizing the "mood" of contemporary black masses. The fandango that Robert Kennedy pulled during May 1963 illustrates this type of misconception about the current Negro upheaval. Bobby Kennedy called in "the leaders" for a friendly chat on what to do about his brother's moral crisis. Baldwin was the most representative of these "leaders." The late Lorraine Hansberry and Lena Horne were others whom the *Times* (May 25, 1963) called "Angry Young Negroes."

First of all, Lena Horne is anything but young! Next, Baldwin and Hansberry were not leading any Negroes. They are great prestige figures, but they have not led any sit-ins, freedom rides, picket lines, street demonstrations, nor have they been beaten over the head by mobs and cops or bitten on the buttocks by dogs. Baldwin, Hansberry, and Lena Horne represent the compassionate type of attitude on the race question. What they do and what they write does not represent an activist, militant point of view, a point of view that more and more Negroes are adopting. If Robert Kennedy wanted to talk to the real leaders of the Negro masses, why did he not summon people who were and are actively involved in the struggle. The only Negro at Robert Kennedy's little tryst who represented the actual leadership of the masses was Jerome Smith. He lives in the South and has been arrested and beaten over the head many times. But no one wanted to listen to him. And Bobby just could not understand why James Baldwin became indignant at this.

The fact that whites automatically assume that Baldwin, because he writes about being black, is a Negro leader, reveals two things: (a) whites are not yet willing to accept the *masses* of Negroes into the mainstream of our society, and (b) whites are still victims of a historic self-deceit by thinking they can hand-pick Negroes who seem to advocate some milkwarm program as leaders, and thereby actually circumvent the true demands and needs of the Negro masses. This is one more reality explaining the white man's "love" for James Baldwin. In large measure, it is this reality that shall wreak more havoc upon the whole of America, south and north.

VI

But what of Baldwin? Has he actually achieved his ambition of becoming a "good writer and an honest man"? I think so. After reading *Another Country*, no one can argue about his honesty, and no critic of the present "literary establishment" would dare deny Baldwin's literary maturity and his complete mastery of the essay form. Recognizing all of this, we must raise the question of why James Baldwin is not satisfied. Why does he continue to bombard the white world with his bleeding words? The answer to this leads back to the reason Baldwin returned to America—to level a ceaseless assault on the forces in this culture that have instilled in him (and all Negroes) an ontological sense of guilt and masculine outrage, all because of black skin. The final "hang-up" must be resolved. In every word Baldwin writes, he is crying for one thing—love, genuine love that, because of having been hated, must involve the quality of humility known as redemption. The essays of James Baldwin constitute a mandate: *white man, we have got to forgive one another once and for all for being black and white, so we can love each other, or our hatred will now destroy us, like a hungry flame!*

In this regard Baldwin is not expressing the "mood" of the masses of Negroes who are, for the most part, concerned with the tangible barriers of their freedom. Baldwin is dealing with the anthropomorphic. Remember, he was a religious man, and obviously still is. In fact, Baldwin very seldom writes about the political, socioeconomic aspects of the Negro question; he does not know that much about sociology or economics. James

Baldwin's protocol is a more spiritual, a more existential exigency. He wants to be rid of the mythlike iniquity that is associated with his blackness, and which plagues his self-esteem incessantly. He does not want to be "tolerated," nor does he want merely to go to bed with our daughters, since such a barbarian notion of his integrity enrages him. He wants MORE, much more than whites ever dreamed of. He wants you, white *man*, to repent and forgive yourself for the nameless horrors you have committed against him and his people. He wants to be *loved* (or appreciated) for his genius and for the gifts of his color to this civilization, with no strings attached. Like any other American, James Baldwin wants to be cleansed "white as snow."

This puts Baldwin in the class with Camus, Sartre, Jaspers, and other existentialists. Baldwin is writing about the blood of the lamb, about sin and redemption. He is perhaps at the categorical head of the newly emerging young black writers, artists and intellectuals in this country that I call existential Negroes.

It is significant for the white man to understand this. At present the white press is making money off James Baldwin, and is congratulating itself on its "liberalness" for publishing and displaying this sweet, nervous black boy. No young Negro can write a book without the publisher sending it to Baldwin to get his imprimatur for advertisements. He is riding on the crest of the commercial literary tide for black writers. There is much speculation among Negroes as to how long this will last, or who will "take Baldwin's place," for we know that historically America has accommodated only *one* Negro writer at a time no matter how many other great ones were around, starving. (This represents one more form of tokenism.) Many fear for Baldwin—"Where will he go from here?" they ask.

I have no such fears. Baldwin will change. He will be forced to. He will massage the white man's conscience less, and become more militant. His exotic style, his perfumed words, will undergo a metamorphosis, or should I say, a turbulent baptism! When this happens, James Baldwin will not be less eloquent but more crude and brute; his pen will begin to draw blood and not merely tears. Already Baldwin has "alarmed" some whites by certain militant statements he has made. Recently he said on the Barry Gray program that he might well prefer Havana to Miami. And since the March on Washington, he has spoken with increasing bitterness and cynicism about national politics on the race problem. In Foley Square (September 22, 1963) he delivered a fiery preachment that made all the others on the platform shake and squirm, including Norman Thomas. Baldwin is beginning to see that the white man in America will never hand over to him what he wants. He (like all Negroes) is going to have to take it by force; perhaps not by violence (I hope) but definitely by coercion. To the extent that this is more and more realized by and demonstrated to Baldwin, his writing will become increasingly similar to Richard Wright's. Ironic? Baldwin was critical of Wright for having too much violence in his work and not enough love. Well, as time goes on (as time does), we may find an increasing quantity and intensity of violence in James Baldwin to the diminishing of sex, or love-making.

When this happens the current romance that whites are carrying on with Baldwin will quietly cease. It is happening already.

A Fiery Baptism

After I finished Blood of the Lamb *I sent it to several American periodicals, all of which returned the manuscript stating that the piece was "very interesting" or that "we liked your article" or that it was "impressive" —BUT! One editor wrote:*

> Thank you for letting us see this interesting analysis. It does not make our peculiar sort of factual piece, however; we are returning it quickly so that you can place it elsewhere.

Another wrote:

> We like your article a good deal, yet we are reluctantly forced to return it to you. Mainly this is due to the fact that the essay by myself to which you refer will be appearing in our very next issue, and two on the same subject would be too much. *Do try us again.*

I put my article under the bed springs and decided to wait. I came to the conclusion that nobody wanted to print my "interesting analysis" not of James Baldwin so much; rather, that they did not care to publish what I had written about the nature of the press and the white public, regarding the nature of this mammoth acceptance of a little, black, "effeminate" man named James Baldwin. And now—after two years have elapsed—I am certain that my conclusion was absolutely correct. Moreover, I am now certain that my "interesting analysis" was and is the most accurate one on the subject that has appeared in print. And finally—now—I want to set the record straight once and for all.

In *Blood Of the Lamb,* I made several analytical predictions. One of these was that Baldwin's writing would undergo a fiery baptism; I also asserted that when this happened the vicarious and pornographic romance that white Americans were carrying on with him would quietly cease.

The truth of my "interesting analysis" was confirmed when James Baldwin wrote his play, *Blues for Mister Charlie,* and by the manner in which the white world reacted to its production. The play was brute, crude, violent, and bold, more in the fashion of Richard Wright (or LeRoi Jones whom I will come to later) than of the usual suffering, pleading, metaphysical Baldwin of *The Fire Next Time* and prior works.

Unlike most plays written by Negroes, *Blues for Mis-*

ter Charlie was not or is not about civil rights or any of
the other "acceptable" subjects on Negro-white relations. The play is based on the Emmett Till murder case
of 1955, and it deals with the sexual variable which is
perhaps the most hushed-up and yet the most explosive
factor involved in racism in the United States. And Baldwin's treatment of it is so straightforward, realistic, and
secular that whites found it difficult to face what they
have been hiding and gliding over for centuries. Moreover, this Baldwin—the *Blues for Mister Charlie* Baldwin—is an aggressive, a masculine Baldwin. Add to this
the fact that the sexuality of the Negroes in the play is
earthy, rich, full of power and human animalism, all of
which Baldwin does not apologize for, but which he af-
firms with dignity and prowess. It was simply too much
for the majority of whites to accept or seriously consider.

For instance, both times I saw the play there were
many, if not more, whites in the audience than there
were Negroes. One could not help but feel the negative
vibrations radiating from the whites throughout the major portion of the evening. They seemed to squirm
throughout the play and grow little in their seats; many
tried to hold a straight face (face of chalk), but one
could see and feel the hot charge boiling beneath their
white masks. Upon two occasions—(a) when Richard
(the Negro hero), back down South telling his friends
how many white girls he has slept with up North and,

showing a photograph of a girl with long hair, remarks, "Man, you know where all that hair's been"; and (b) when Richard tells Lyle, (the southern bigot) who has been threatening him, "Man, are you scared I'm going to get in your wife's drawers?"—I thought half of the white audience might jump up and storm out of the theatre. But they held onto their seats. Again, after Richard has been murdered by Lyle, and Juanita (Richard's sweetheart, Diana Sands) in lamentation delivers her speech on how Richard made love to her, describing it in plain but powerful language, telling how she took Richard into her womb and how she "grind" him and how meaningful the act was—again, I saw the theatre faces of white people twist and contort in agony and revulsion. In fact, the white ladies sitting next to me began gossiping very rapidly about the careers of Rip Torn (Lyle) and Pat Hingle (Parnell, the southern liberal) as if nothing was happening on stage at all. And the applauding of the whites—one got the impression that it was as much out of nervous reaction to cover up embarrassment as it was an expression of honest enthusiasm.

On the other hand, Negroes seemed to be enthralled with delight and moral vindication to see for the first time the true nature of their lives, and their plight, played back to them with dignity and no beating around the bush. Many Negroes were there with white companions. I recall one tall dark Negro who is a famous

man. He came in with his white girl and sat down as if
he was out for the usual "high-brow" theatre evening.
Before the play was half through, the Negro had unbut-
toned his collar, had reared back in his seat, and was
looking around as if he himself had written *Blues for
Mister Charlie*. Pride was bursting on his face and chest.

Not only did whites in general recoil from the play,
but the press, in most cases, reviewed something other
than what the play was. The majority of reviewers said
the play failed as a "civil rights" play. Those few who
admitted what the play was about found ways of debunk-
ing it as far-fetched, saying that Richard got lynched because he "asked for it" (*The Village Voice*, April 30,
1964). Only one reviewer wrote a favorable piece about
the play. His name is Tom Driver and he has since re-
signed mysteriously from *The Reporter*. His favorable
review was not printed in the magazine.

What Tom Driver said in his review (which was eventually published in the *Negro Digest*, *Voice*, and *Chris-
tianity and Crisis*) was that the *virtues* of the play killed
it. He praised the language of the play, which was raw,
earthy, and full of four letter words (and caused whites
to shiver in their seats). After lauding Diana Sands's role
as the "best performance any American actress has given
this year," Driver went on to affirm the essential reality
of what the play was about: that the white man (and
woman) in America has a sexual "hang-up" about him-

self *vis-à-vis* the Negro, and it is this hang-up that ter-
rifies the white man whenever he encounters the Negro
and causes so much violence and bloodshed. Most of all,
Driver viewed favorably Baldwin's stereotyped projection
of southern Negroes and whites; that is, the "sterile and
sexually insecure" white male who places his "lily-white"
wife upon a pedestal while he slips around at night with
Negro women, and the "virile and lusty" Negro who
enjoys the sex act to the fullest without guilt or reservations. Parnell, the southern liberal, confesses on stage
his deep sexual involvement with a Negro woman. Lyle,
the southern bigot who is so afraid that Richard is after
his wife, brags about how he has taken the bodies of
many Negro girls. In fact, Lyle is really interested in
Richard's sweetheart Miss Sands, rather than the other
way around. And Jo (Lyle's wife, brilliantly played by
Ann Wedgeworth), the typical fragile and neglected
southern "lady" who usually knows about her husband's
clandestine behavior with black women and who herself has come to accept all the stereotyped notions and
emotions about and toward the Negro, leaps (almost
gladly!) to comply with her husband's accusation that
Richard has "attacked" her when the latter came to
Lyle's store to buy a Coke. In reality Richard never
touched the woman and the woman knows it; yet in court
she testifies to the contrary, and Lyle is set free *for* mur-

dering Richard, after which Lyle brags again, "Hell yes, I killed that nigger," and is glad of it.

We "liberals" in America always want justice to win out in the end. Well, in the South there is no justice when it comes to the Negro. And Baldwin wrote it as it really is. The murderers of countless Emmett Tills are still running amuck throughout the entire South.

As I have indicated, many of the reviewers accused Baldwin of not writing a play, "technically" speaking. Well now, several of the plays of Arthur Miller, Eugene O'Neill, Clifford Odets, and others (*The Deputy*, for instance) are not plays, "technically" speaking. Yet such plays enjoy successful runs on, as well as off, Broadway. Any art form, I say art *form*, that deals with man's inhumanity to man and does not end with "justice winning out" or "crime does not pay," is viewed and reviewed in America as "controversial." Let's come closer to home. In regards to the Negro, when the white man is portrayed as a barbarous, unmitigated bigot, we not only label the art form as "controversial," we also cry out that it is not "art"; we call it "propaganda." Specifically, *Blues for Mister Charlie* hits white America between the eyes, and does not apologize for doing so. Evidently, to talk about the white man's sexual fears and guilts is to strike him in the most vulnerable corners of his ego. And he loses all rationality, all objectivity. He either goes blank or he tries to absolve his guilt by simple-minded rationalizations. For instance, Michael Smith (*Voice*, April 30, 1964) claims, ". . . Lyle kills Richard not so much because he is a Negro as because he asks for it." Later Smith asserts, "Lyle, more in defense of his sex-self-respect than of his race, murders Richard."

Unfortunately (or is it fortunately?) these remarks reveal more about Mr. Smith than they do about *Blues for Mister Charlie*. First of all, Richard does not behave around whites (Lyle and his wife) according to the "bowing-and-scraping" pattern that bigoted whites demand in the South. No, Richard walks and talks like a man who is aware of his dignity and inherent equality as a human being. To the psychotic white in the South this takes on a sexual meaning, it is perceived as sexual assault. Secondly, the only sexual self-respect Lyle has is a false one, a guilty one shot through with, and based on, white male supremacy! Doesn't Mr. Smith know that sexual guilt and paranoia are intricate aspects of racism in America? James Baldwin does! And thirdly, if Richard is "mean and tormented and looking for trouble," *why* is he mean, by *what* is he tormented? But most of all, Mr. Smith, similar to his southern counterpart, seems to interpret Richard's "talking-back" and standing up to Lyle and his wife as "looking for trouble."

I suppose that great numbers of Negroes in the South today are standing up and talking back and demanding human respect and in the process are "looking for trouble." I suppose that endeavoring to secure their God-given rights and seeking to make America a better place in which ALL Americans can live, means, with reference to their lynching, that Medgar Evers and James Chaney and countless others, "asked for it." And finally, while throughout the decades the sexuality as well as the general behavior traits of Negroes have been thought of and portrayed as vulgar, subhuman and derogative, it is a telling thing that only when these same traits are portrayed with prowess and dignity against the barbarity, both sexual and otherwise, of whites, that only then (only now!) white men rise up to shout down intrusions. My grandmother used to say, "the ones who yell the loudest is the culprits with the mostest to hide."

In fact, there seemed to have been, at one time or another, an inside move to kill *Blues for Mister Charlie* before it came to its natural end, if its end was indeed natural. One day, an editor of a New York magazine called the box office for ticket reservations and was told by one person that all seats were sold out. The same editor waited several hours and called again, for he had been told such would happen, and, behold, he was informed this time by another person that there were plenty of tickets available. I also understand that someone significantly connected with the play was quoted as having said: "Before I will have the things said about white men that are being said upon that stage, I'd soon as go broke."

Now what does all this mean in terms of Baldwin's development as a writer and as a Negro? First, as a writer, he is no longer addressing a predominantly white audience, at least no longer in the guilt-soothing terms that characterized most of his previous essays. In *Blues for Mister Charlie,* he was no longer dealing exclusively with the subjective or moral coefficients of the white world's inhumanity toward the Negro. Rather, Baldwin was dealing with the raw, brute, objective *facts* of the white man's barbarity toward black people in America. Along with the terrible facts, there are the white man's fears, anxieties, and most of all, his guilt! *Blues for Mister Charlie* cut and plowed deep into the very psyche of white America and, with justified animosity and vindictiveness, hurled all of his atrocious deeds and horrible guilts, solidly back into the white man's face! And, seemingly, it is, and was, too much for whites to bear. But Negroes loved it.

Which means that Baldwin, as a Negro, is writing less to soothe white folk's guilt and more to enlighten, dignify and anger American Negroes. With *Blues for Mister Charlie,* Baldwin plunged into the position of being a true spokesman not just for the middle class but for the *masses* of his people. Michael Smith of the *Voice* made this observation and added that it was "unfortunate," claiming that being a spokesman for the Negro nearly prevented Baldwin from being an "artist." Why is it that, after the production of *Blues for Mister Charlie* appeared, the very same whites who used to praise Baldwin now rise up to put him down!

Baldwin is not merely a writer. He is a Negro writer, and we, especially *white* Americans, have seen to that and no doubt will continue to see to it for a long time hence. The *fact* that *Blues for Mister Charlie* was or is *artistically* a bad play is about as relevant to the real issue as saying that *Crime and Punishment* is artistically a bulky, sloppy novel, which it certainly is. To wit, *Another Country* is so bad artistically that I am relatively sure its publication had little to do with art. But the critics "raved." They did not talk about the artistry of the book, but how "bold" it was. With drooling mouths the public consumed it to the ticker tape of the best-seller lists. I saw them on subways, on buses, at lunch counters and mid-town Madison Avenue restaurants—especially the young, up-and-coming, clean-shaven, no-mustached, gray-flanneled. Coming and going, I saw them reading about the country of A-not-her! Talk about art vs. propaganda. *Another Country* was almost nothing but propaganda; and let's face it, propaganda for homosexualism. I am definitely not making a moral judgment about homosexualism, as artistic subject matter, or about James Baldwin. I am making a moral analysis of the character structure of white Americans regarding their good faith when it comes to facing up to the social, political, economic and sexual horrors, in artistic presentations as well as in reality, that have and are being heaped upon the American Negro. It seems, and this is the *real* issue, that whites in *this* country, despite an abundance of liberalism, are not yet morally capable of accepting any open presentation of, on the one hand, their sexual feelings regarding black men, and on the other hand, the guilt stemming from and the fact of the sexual depravity that white men (especially southerners) have historically inflicted upon Negro women. This is what killed *Blues for Mister Charlie* and, in my opinion, severed the romantic involvement between James Baldwin and white America, forever.

Although James Baldwin might not sell as many books and will not be so affectionately discussed in white circles, or for that matter in lily-nice, middle-class Negro circles, the cessation of the romance represents a step forward rather than a stumble backward. Characteristically, Baldwin has written of the race problem, or of Negro-white relations, with a deep burning *love* (submission) that was rooted in the religion of the long-suffering. Repeatedly, incessantly, James Baldwin has pleaded with passion for forgiveness and love between whites and blacks as the solution for the nightmare that makes havoc of our lives. But, I believe, it has become apparent to Baldwin that the probability of a cleansing love and forgiveness between Negroes and whites is long in forthcoming. America is one of the most spiritually bankrupt countries in a world where it is, as Baldwin must know by now, terribly difficult to create and maintain a *personal* love, let alone love of mankind. But this is not to say that we will no longer see in Baldwin's work the influence of a deeply religious man. Emile Capouya, a former editor at Macmillan who once shared an apartment with Baldwin, pointed out in 1963 during a lecture at the New School for Social Research that James Baldwin is not really a deep thinker in the sense of an academic or even a rugged intellectual; rather, he is a provincial preacher with a grand intelligence for literary style and eloquence—and he is at his best, as can be seen by comparing his essays with his fiction, when he is writing out of the depths of his spiritual background. And this background will continue to echo in his labor—no matter how charged otherwise with secular rage—until he lays his pen down and saunters into elemental peace.

One final contention must be resolved. While James Baldwin was being called, with reference to the race problem, the "conscience of the nation," I wrote that as a Negro writer he stood at the head of a group of emerging black artists and writers, in particular those whom I called, "the Existential Negroes." When I made that statement I failed to point out several things. First of all, Baldwin's existentialism is rooted in religion, in spirituality, in the metaphysical. This means: (a) in analyzing the race problem, Baldwin has dwelt primarily with aspects such as *hate, anguish, guilt, conscience, internal torture, sin,* and *iniquity*—his favorite term, I believe, is a word which applies a "riddle" or a "mystery" to race relations: *conundrum;* (b) when it comes to alleviating the race problem his key terms include such concepts as *love, redemption, cleansing the heart, forgiveness, endurance,* and so on. If the elements of a situation are viewed in religious terms, then it follows that the resolution of the situation must come in and through religious measures, such as, for instance, "forgiveness."

Specifically, James Baldwin is a *religious* existentialist. His task, whether he intended it or not, has been, as it were, to clear the air of all moral or metaphysical issues and cobwebs, and to define, in the realm of spirituality, what must be done to end the nightmare of our lives. Notice, he always speaks in terms of "our"—which is to say, both white and Negro.

Baldwin has performed (and only God knows how!) his task excellently. He has made our hearts tremble, his words have filled us with compassion, and the genius of his consternation has enthralled and whiplashed our consciences. In a word, James *The Fire Next Time* Baldwin has caused us to weep. But beyond this nothing more has ensued. And that is as it should be, for, as we all know, Americans have a peculiar kind of religion where we go to church on Sunday and weep and confess our guilts, only to go the rest of the week and commit the same crimes. But do not play Baldwin cheap. He has, perhaps inadvertently, proved his point masterfully —no amount of mere preaching is going to cause white people to go out in the real world and undo the objective sociopolitical and economic conditions which they have instituted in order to prevent the Negro from realizing the fruits of American democracy. And the awareness of this has inspired, has *necessitated*, on the part of other Negro writers, the assumption of a secular rather than religious frame of reference when handling subject matter that deals with the race problem. These writers—no matter what they say—owe James Baldwin, as he owes Richard Wright, a great deal. But let's get to them.

The *secular* or *non-religious* existential black artists, especially the writers, do not deal in the metaphysical or the moral abstractions of race relations. They deal with the brute facts of oppression, with murder, lynching, discrimination, segregation, castration, riot, bloodshed! They do not speak of "love," "forgiveness," "cleansing the heart," or any of the rest. They speak of revenge— *black* revenge! They "run things down" in terms of the "nitty-gritty"; they are not worried about the "art" of their calling; they employ terms such as "motherfucker" "white sonsofbitches" whenever they feel the need to do so, which is very often. Unlike Baldwin, they are not ashamed of eating watermelon or collard greens or any of the other "soul" foods. They are not troubled by the fact that Negroes have not produced a Rembrandt; many of them conceive of their work as being far better than Rembrandt. And while many other writers such as Baldwin write to and for white audiences, which restricts their works in scope, power, and aggressiveness according to what they think whites will accept, the black writers in question may write *to* white people, but what they are saying is *for* Negroes.

Specifically I have in mind LeRoi Jones. Not so much in his poetry, although certainly it is there too, but in his fiction, drama, criticism and scholarly works there is but one constant hammering—to be BLACK in America is to be REVOLUTIONARY. In *Dutchman, The Toilet,* as well as in *The Slave,* three plays by LeRoi Jones, there is all the hatred, venom, brutality, profanity, and downright insanity that whites have traditionally heaped upon the Negro, but now turned back upon whites. Whitman once said, "A poet enlisted in a people's cause can make every word he writes draw blood." Jones, and those gathered about him, are not begging white society to love them. No. They are out to *take* their freedom and dignity as black men and to harass the white world while, at the same time, inspiring the black masses of Negroes to the affirmation of their inherent beauty and worth, not as middle-class-oriented integrated Negroes, but as Black People.

With slightly less emphasis on "blackism," the same may be said of writers and poets such as Harold Cruse, Ishmael Reed, and David Henderson, and a few others who are associated with the magazine *Umbra*. All these men are talented and young. They do not write lily-word sonnets. Their works are affluent with the kind of language that smacks of the brute exigencies of day-to-day Negro life in America. Distinctively, as opposed to James Baldwin and others like him, I call these writers "Secular Existential Negro Writers."

But it is LeRoi Jones who stands, for the present at least, as the master of these writers and of the movement. The white literary establishment (along with the literate public) is reacting to him in mixed fashion—with praise, sensationalism, and awe, on the one hand, and with caution, castigation, and absolute "put-down," on the other. Of the first instance, the *Herald Tribune* magazine has called Jones the "King of the Lower East Side." Of the second instance, Richard Elman, in his review of *The Dead Lecturer* which appeared in the *New York Times Book Review* wanted to know why Jones always talked about hating white people, and he accused Jones of not being an "artist," calling for the "real" Mr. Jones to come forward. In still further instances, not only are a great many white critics putting Jones down for being an "anti-racist-racist" (whatever that is!) rather than a "true artist" (whatever that is, also!), but some white establishment-oriented Negroes are finding excuses to put him down also—Ralph Ellison, for instance, in reviewing Jones's *Blues People*, a brilliant study on the origin and development of the blues, side-lashed Jones with the cute remark that Jones's sociological treatment of the blues would "give the blues the blues." Well, with reference to Ellison, his negative remarks seemed to be prompted more by overcriticism than by the facts of the book. The case is clear with Elman—before he could call Jones an artist he wanted to hear Jones say: "White man, I love you."

In the midst of all this—the sensationalism and the put-downs—I discern a hazard if not a trap for LeRoi Jones, first as a creative writer and second as a Negro concerned in his work and in his life about the situation of black people in America. Jones is running two risks. In America it is so easy, because of the Hollywood interpretation of success and the universalization of commercialism, for a dynamic and talented artist and his works, no matter how seriously rendered, to be expropriated as a "show" for the sensationalistic appetite that seems to characterize the American public. For a Negro this is doubly true. What ensues is the making of the individual artist into a cult. And, make no mistake, it does not matter who does it or for what reasons, a cult is short-lived; but more important is the fact that when somebody or something makes one into a cult, it is for the function of eventually destroying (sacrificing) the individual around whom the cult has risen.

Finally, creative brilliance and unmitigatable convictions are no guarantees against insanity. In fact, the entire spectrum of the Negro-white situation in America is littered with persons and forces that pull toward psychopathy. And this is a thing that the talented Negro artist, who is bitterly but authentically involved in or concerned with the destruction of the racist nightmare in America, should watch with the vigilance of a Mahatma Gandhi.

CHAPTER 5

STRANGER IN BABYLON

REFLECTIONS ON THE MARCH ON WASHINGTON

I cannot speak for the thousands of black and white men and women who converged on the capital of our nation, August 28, 1963. I can only speak for myself. I assume that thousands saw what I saw and heard what I heard. The thing that troubled me, however, was what I *felt*.

I know there is no going on a journey naked. Perhaps my mood was due to something I ate, something I drank, smoked? Maybe it was due to the sense of guilt (failure) that has plagued me for the last year because, having made up my mind to succeed as a writer or not to succeed at all, I have seemingly set about destroying myself, and have definitely hurt others whom I love and respect. I do not know specifically what caused me to feel the things

I felt. All I know is I felt them. As I stepped from the train, walking with the crowd through the station, out into the city of Washington, a terrible dread—an ominous presence—settled upon me. Forbodedom! Not so much for the march per se, or any single thing by itself, but for a total civilization.

When I say "total civilization," I mean Babylon. During the days of the persecution of the Hebrews, the topography of Babylon must have looked like that of Washington, D.C. The oblong, granite structures that line Independence and Constitution avenues symbolized and contained the naked power, money, and glory of our nation. Something struck me as awesome about these hard, crisp edifices behind whose pseudo-Grecian portals the dreams and fears of two hundred million Americans are manufactured and regulated into just so many vertical and horizontal echelons of cold bureaucracy. And I could not put away the feeling that we were something like the Hebrew children walking in the splendid but foredoomed city that was Babylon.

And we, especially those of us who were black, had journeyed to the center of our civilization to protest three centuries of slavery. We had come to express our impatience, our militancy about a democracy that has taken so much of our sweat, blood, and tears, but which has denied us the right to the fruits therefrom. We had converged on Washington to demonstrate—peaceably, but

definitely—our *disobedience* to the mores of inhumanity
characteristic of our lot.

I kept thinking that these were the reasons we had
come to the capital of our lives. But, as the day lulled on
in the heat of late August, and the various activities
transpired, I grew haunted with the feeling that few, if
any, of these things were really happening. Something
was wrong. I looked around me. The streets and grounds
were heavy-laden with multitudes. And then I saw something else. The militia! Cops and soldiers were everywhere. Their faces were stern and cold. Their guns were
ready in their holsters, and in their firm hands were
the big black sticks. Trucks and jeeps and walkie-talkies.
I felt whatever people feel when they are in captivity.
The military was spaced out in strategic places, on top
of buildings, at high vantage points with telescopes and
rifles; jets flying so low as to drown out the speakers.
We were under total surveillance! A feeling of loneli-
ness swept over me. For, I felt, although we were there
in thousands, we were not *with* one another, we were
among one another. The multitude appeared to be an
aggregate and not a congregate. We were things to be
acted upon rather than actors ourselves. We were orated
to, sung to, directed here and there, thoroughly policed,
and then ushered back on trains, planes, and buses, out
of the city.

Had it not been planned this way? Had not the leaders

met with the President, and been told what we could and could not do? Had not the *protest* ingredient of the march been negotiated and pre-structured right out of the whole affair? I wondered.

And as I wondered, I thought about the astounding number of people who had turned out. Everywhere there were thousands upon thousands. Perhaps the mere physical presence of numbers bespoke militancy. No doubt it did. Yet the word alienation, the word *estrangement* kept running around in my mind. I felt we were there in great numbers, but only as individual small groups connected by common concerns, and not as one great congregation tied together and moved by the force of actively participating in, or exchanging awareness of, what was going on. There were so many people, and the whole thing was such a colossus, that not one-third of us could actually witness, by ear or vision, much of what was going on. I, for one, found it impossible to push through the numbers to see at least one of the principals. And there were so many white faces among us, marching, cheer-leading, and trying to sing Negro spirituals. I have no particular dislike for white people; I know some whites have always aided the Negro in his struggle for freedom. Still, I wondered and do wonder—what was the meaning of all those white faces in Washington? Whatever the meaning, I know it had a profound effect on me; and I know also that it had a crucial effect upon the future of the Negro's struggle for freedom in America.

Of all that went on, only three things stirred my soul that day: the mighty, indomitable voice of Mahalia Jackson; the pseudo-Whitmanlike oratory of Dr. King; and the announcement that the flaming torch of the great torchbearer, Dr. W. E. B. DuBois, had finally, after almost a century of setting our hearts on fire, succumbed to darkness. When I heard the announcement I sat on the ground. Behind my sunglasses tears flooded my eyes. It came upon me that the most significant thing for all two hundred thousand of us to do at that moment would be to kneel on the grounds, the streets and sidewalks, and for one hour, let no sound be made or uttered. Instead, a diffused sigh came from a portion of the crowd that heard the news. That was all.

Other than these three incidents, plus the initial enthusiasm of the people on the train down from New York, the March on Washington, however significant, was a bore to me. I hazard to say it was a bore to a lot of people, a sort of surrealistic disillusionment which seemed to elude conscious recognition. Perhaps I am a victim of hallucination, but it seemed that a host of people were asleep on the grounds. Others were buying souvenirs and mementos, as if they were at a carnival. Many spread boxes and ate picnic-style. I saw people applauding when they had heard not one word of what the speaker uttered. And still others were taking in the sights like tourists, or were playing radios to find out what was going on right there under their noses. Many of us were plain tired from the long trip. And most of these things could not be helped.

But let me return to Babylon. The king, Nebuchadnezzar, built an idol of gold, and it was the living embodiment of what Babylonian civilization stood for in those days. The idol of gold was Babylon's god, and the king decreed that upon the sounding of three gongs, everybody must bow down to the golden god. I know it is the nature of men to erect edifices to themselves, to make visual and concrete symbols of the values that rule their lives. Americans are no exception. Yet I am disturbed over the thoughts that flooded my being when, standing there in the crowd, I looked up and saw the Washington Monument. At first I think I was frightened. It was so tall and monolithic, so un-alive and, at once, so totally captivating.

I do not know what the monument has to do with George Washington; I know, however, it has everything to do with the supreme *de facto* value of our nation, the value that has made America so materially great and yet so spiritually impoverished. I am talking about *money*. This is what the Washington Monument symbolizes to me. It is a cold, callous, inorganic thing. It is architecturally ugly. It is an artifact phallus, ejaculating the impersonality of its technographic erection up at God's omnipresent horizon. We were helpless and infinitely small, scattered there beneath it on the grounds.

If that edifice has something to do with the founding of this republic, if it symbolizes the blood and sweat and spirit with which America wrested the clutches of England from around her neck and lifted this country to a free nation, then it seems to me to be a hard and eerie thing that after some three hundred years there are still within this great land over twenty million men and women whose condition is worse, *much* worse than in colonial times prior to the ordeal which gave us glory to erect a monument.

I hope and pray that my feelings are wrong about the Washington Monument. But if I am largely correct, if we have forgotten the values (if we ever had them) for which it was lifted high, then I would give my life to see ALL Americans—Negroes and whites—in freedom and passion for one another, lift *ourselves* above that lifeless thing. What America needs most now is *room*, a kind of transcendent humanity, whereby all men and women can work, love and acquire self-esteem without having to maim one another in the struggle. We need a deliberate zeal, religious in intensity, for the mastery of the grammar and vanity of our egos, and that, to my mind, requires organic changes in our total civilization.

New York, 1965

DATE DUE

1-3			
MAR 31 1969			
GAYLORD			PRINTED IN U.S.A.